# The Gem Set in Gold

a manual of pariyatti
containing the Pāli and Hindi chanting
from a ten-day course of Vipassana Meditation

by S. N. Goenka

Vipassana Research Publications

Vipassana Research Publications
(an imprint of)
Pariyatti Publishing
www.pariyatti.org

First Edition 2006
PDF eBook 2012



ISBN: 978-1-928706-29-8 (paperback)
ISBN: 978-1-938754-05-0 (PDF eBook)
ISBN: 978-1-938754-14-2 (ePub)
ISBN: 978-1938754-15-9 (Mobi)

Library of Congress Control Number: 2006929680

*Gāravo ca nivāto ca,*
*santuṭṭhi ca kataññutā;*
*kālena dhammassavanaṃ,*
*etaṃ maṅgalamuttamaṃ.*

Respectfulness, humility,
contentment, gratitude,
listening to the Dhamma at the proper time
this is the highest welfare.

—*Gotama Buddha*
*Maṅgala Suttaṃ*

For a Vipassana meditator the literature of Pāli is a storehouse of Dhamma; so sweet like a cake prepared with honey it is sweet everywhere. Every word is full of ambrosia . . . I am sure this language is going to become very much alive.

—*S. N. Goenka*

# Contents

## Introduction

In 1969, S. N. Goenka, the revered teacher of Vipassana meditation, left his homeland, Myanmar (Burma), to travel to India. At that time Myanmar customs officials were especially vigilant about the smuggling of precious jewels out of the country. At the Yangon airport, Goenkaji was asked if he was carrying any valuables with him. He smilingly replied, "I am carrying a gem." He went on to explain to the concerned official, "The gem I am taking from here will be used to pay back a debt of Myanmar to India. It originally came from India, and is sorely needed there today. By my taking it from here, Myanmar will not be any poorer. I am taking the jewel of the Dhamma."

This jewel, the sublime practical teaching of the Buddha, has now been given to people throughout the world. Carefully preserved for centuries in the small country of Myanmar, it has, under Goenkaji's compassionate and energetic guidance, returned to India, its source, and from there has spread to the rest of the world. Tens of thousands of people from a vast spectrum of cultures, religions and nationalities, have started walking on this ancient path, to free themselves from the bondage of suffering.

The treasure which Goenkaji has been distributing is Vipassana, the quintessence of the Buddha's teaching. As he imparts the jewel of the practice, using his own words, in languages current in today's world, he also encourages the study of the original teaching of the Buddha in *his* own language: Pāli. In Pāli these two complementary aspects of Dhamma are known as *paṭipatti* and *pariyatti*. Goenkaji refers to these as, "a gem, the beauty of which is enhanced by its golden setting."

As a teacher, Goenkaji has always given primary importance to *paṭipatti*, the practical aspect, because it is only the experience of truth through systematic self-introspection that can purify the mind and relieve suffering. This is the gem of the Dhamma. Hand in hand with the practice of meditation, however, is the theoretical foundation, like the protective golden setting for a valuable gem. The firm foundation of *pariyatti* provides the necessary guidance and inspiration for practitioners to take, and keep taking, proper steps on the Path.

Fortunately for our generation and those that follow, S. N. Goenka is a master of both *pariyatti* and *paṭipatti*. Indeed, when he came to India in 1969, he brought both aspects of the Dhamma with him—not only his unique capacity to teach meditation, but also literally hundreds of texts of the Tipiṭaka, the Buddhist Pāli scriptures, in Burmese script.

The decades since have seen the ripening of these two aspects. Thousands of seekers have come to ten-day Vipassana courses in various parts of the world to experience first-hand the transformative effects of Dhamma—to put the Buddha's words into practice, and start to emerge from suffering. And through the publications of the Vipassana Research Institute (founded in 1985) meditators have been able to study the Buddha's words and practice at a much deeper level.

Goenkaji's rare ability to explain the Buddha's teaching is deeply enhanced by his proficiency in several languages, including Pāli. Pāli is the language in which the Buddha taught, and in which his teachings have been preserved. As with Sanskrit and Latin, it is not a contemporary spoken language, but a so-called "dead language"—a medium, nevertheless, conveying and illuminating a living tradition.

Pāli is unique in many ways. One of the meanings of the word Pāli is "that which protects, or preserves." Pāli exists to preserve the words of the enlightened person, Gotama Buddha. The tradition is that, by expressing the sublime teaching which allows beings to be liberated from the rounds of suffering, Pāli protects the people; it preserves the invaluable treasure of the Buddha's own words.

Adherence to the use of the Buddha's language has been a profoundly significant part of the living tradition handed down in the Theravāda Buddhist countries, which have preserved Pāli in its oldest form. Faithfulness to the Pāli words of the Buddha has therefore been a central part of the teaching of S. N. Goenka, and the lineage which he represents.

Students at Vipassana courses practice meditation in a special environment—one where the highest merits of *pariyatti* and *paṭipatti* are conjoined. The meditators undertake the delicate and demanding task of examining their own minds in a surrounding which intermingles long stretches of silent introspection with periods of instruction, conveyed by Goenkaji's recorded words in Hindi or English. Students of these courses are familiar with Goenkaji's use of Pāli in the daily discourses (in which he explains the theory of the meditation technique), as well as in his practice of chanting both the Buddha's words and his own inspiring compositions, rhymed Hindi couplets known as *dohas*.

Dhamma teachers have different modes of expression. For Goenkaji (who is a poet and orator in his native languages of Rajasthani and Hindi), his melodic use of Pāli and Hindi *dohas* is a medium through which his abundant *mettā* (feelings of goodwill towards all beings) is conveyed. When he chants in Pāli, or in his native tongues, along with the sounds of his resonant voice come waves of compassion and loving-kindness. This provides a congenial, supportive atmosphere in which the Dhamma can be received and practiced.

For many years, meditators have wanted to understand the meaning of the words chanted by Goenkaji during a ten-day course. *The Gem Set in Gold* is the first thorough compilation of these words of Dhamma, and their translation into English. This compilation is, in fact, a link to all the successive generations of meditators from the exalted time of the Buddha to the present, who preserved the technique in its pristine purity.

While impressive as *pariyatti*—a rich collection of inspirational passages from the Buddha and a contemporary Dhamma teacher of rare qualities—it is in conjunction with the actual practice that this volume lives up to its name. Students who hear Goenkaji's chanting at a Vipassana course do so in the rarefied environment of a deep meditation course where they are putting the Buddha's words into practice. Those who read them will understand their meaning and be able to apply them much more deeply in the context of their meditation practice.

May *The Gem Set in Gold* benefit many generations, and help to fulfill Goenkaji's exhortation: "Our aim is always to experience the Dhamma within ourselves in order to emerge from all suffering. The means to do so is the practice of Vipassana meditation. Reading, writing and study are merely to find guidance and inspiration in order to go more deeply in the practice, and thus to come closer to the goal of liberation."

## A Note about the Chanting

The various occasions during a ten-day course when S. N. Goenka chants are standard in all recordings of the instructions. The chanting that is presented here is taken from the Hindi-English course set, recorded at Dhamma Giri, Igatpuri, India, in 1985. Since this is also the set of instructions used for translation into all languages other than the languages Goenkaji teaches in, Hindi and English, it is also the international standard set. There are a few minor variations of the Hindi *dohas* in the English-only instruction set that was recorded at Dhamma Dharā, in Massachusetts, USA, in 1984. Since these are few and minor we have not noted these variations, so as to avoid further complication of the text.

The Pāli *suttas* that are heard at dawn during the morning chanting each day have various sources. The short note at the beginning of each day's *sutta* text gives a brief explanation of the text and where it is found in the Pāli literature, if possible. Several of the daily "*suttas*" are not actually found in the canonical Pāli Tipiṭaka. They are traditional *paritta*s, or protective chantings, that have been preserved for centuries and have become a standard part of daily devotional practice in the Theravāda countries.

This *paritta* tradition is a very old one, dating back to the time of the Buddha himself. In the *Dīgha-nikāya*, at the end of the *Āṭānāṭiya Sutta*, the Buddha exhorts the monks, "*Bhikkhus*, you should learn these Āṭānāṭa protective verses, master them and remember them. They are for your benefit and, through them, *Bhikkhus* and *bhikkhunis,* male and female lay followers may live guarded, protected, unharmed and at ease." In another place, in the *Vinaya-piṭaka (Cūḷavagga, 5)*, the Buddha teaches the monks the *Khandha-paritta* as a way to give *mettā* to snakes and other wild creatures in order to provide protection from being harmed by them.

With these beginnings from the oldest sources, over time there came to be an established collection of *paritta*, or protective verses, for different occasions. Some are taken from the canonical literature, but often an introductory verse was composed and added later. Others were compilations of inspirational verses each of which referred to events or *suttas* from the Pāli canon. There are examples of all of these types among the morning chanting collection here.

The chanting that opens and closes the daily group sittings features Goenkaji's *dohas*. These *dohas* and their translation have long been available in the booklet *Come People of the World*. Our attempt in this book has been to give a complete compilation of all the chanting, both Hindi and Pāli, that a Vipassana student hears in the ten-day course. These *dohas* are reprinted here in that spirit.

Many of the Pāli passages from the evening discourses that are compiled in the last chapter are also chanted at some time, or perhaps every day, during the morning chanting. We have included this chapter, despite the obvious redundancy, in order to provide readers with a handy reference to passages they may hear in the discourses.

Goenkaji's discourses have been recorded several times and in various locations during the decades in which he has been teaching. At different times and places he has quoted different Pāli passages from the Buddha's teaching to illustrate his points in the discourses. There tended to be more Pāli quoted in the early period of his teaching career. Later on, as he began teaching in the West, certain passages were eliminated altogether, or the translation may have been given without his actually reciting the Pāli. The Pāli presented here in the chapter of passages heard in the discourses is from the English discourse set, recorded at Dhamma Mahāvana, California, USA, in 1991.

We have tried to present translations that carry the spirit of the original language and that follow the text reasonably closely, word for word and line by line, so someone with little Pāli, or no Hindi, can read along and draw connections between a particular word or phrase in the original and its English meaning. In order to maintain reasonable English grammar this has not been possible for every line of translation, however.

For anyone who would like to study the Pāli more carefully, there is an appendix with individual word meanings for many of the key Pāli texts recited during the morning chanting sessions. This is not intended to be a comprehensive grammar or textbook. It should, however, help a reader who is studying Pāli to follow the translation more carefully in conjunction with one of the various Pāli textbooks available in the market.

*the editors*
*VRI, Dhamma Giri, 2006*

## Pāli and Hindi Pronunciation

**The Pāli alphabet** consists of forty-one characters: eight vowels and thirty-three consonants.

**Vowels:** a, ā, i, ī, u, ū, e, o

**Consonants:**

| | | | | | |
|---|---|---|---|---|---|
| Velar: | k | kh | g | gh | ṅ |
| Palatal: | c | ch | j | jh | ñ |
| Retroflex: | ṭ | ṭh | ḍ | ḍh | ṇ |
| Dental: | t | th | d | dh | n |
| Labial: | p | ph | b | bh | m |
| Miscellaneous: | y, r, l, v, s, h, ḷ, ṃ | | | | |

The vowels **a, i, u** are short; **ā, ī, ū** are long; **e** and **o** are of middle length. They are pronounced short before double consonants: *mettā, khetta, koṭṭha, sotthi*; and long before single consonants: *devā, senā; loka, odana*.

**a** is pronounced like 'a' in 'about';
**ā** like 'a' in 'father';
**i** is pronounced like 'i' in 'mint';
**ī** like 'ee' in 'see';
**u** is pronounced like 'u' in 'put';
**ū** like 'oo' in 'pool'.

The consonant **c** is soft, pronounced as in the 'ch' in 'church'. All the aspirated consonants are pronounced with an audible expulsion of breath following the normal unaspirated sound. Therefore **th** is not as in 'three' but more like the sound in 'Thailand', and **ph** is not as in 'photo' but rather is pronounced 'p' accompanied by an expulsion of breath.

The retroflex consonants, **ṭ, ṭh, ḍ, ḍh, ṇ** are pronounced with the tip of the tongue turned back, whereas in the dentals, **t, th, d, dh, n,** it touches the upper front teeth.

The palatal nasal, ñ, is the same as the Spanish 'ñ', as in señor. The velar nasal, ṅ, is pronounced like 'ng' in 'singer' but occurs only with the other consonants in its group: *ṅk, ṅkh, ṅg, ṅgh*. The pronunciation of ṃ is similar to ṅ but occurs most commonly as a terminal nasalization: '*evaṃ me sutaṃ*'. The Pāli v is a soft 'v' or 'w' and *ḷ*, produced with the tongue retroflexed, is almost a combined 'rl' sound.

**The Hindi alphabet** uses all the same characters as Pāli except **ḷ**. There are also an additional four vowels and two more consonants:

**Vowels:** ai, au, ḥ, ṛ

**Consonants:** ś, ṣ

The vowels represented by the diphthongs **ai,** and **au** are pronounced as they would be in English: **ai** like 'aee' and **au** like the 'ou' in 'loud.'

(Note that, in Hindi transliteration to Roman script, **ie** and **ae** are not dipthongs; in each case the two vowels are pronounced separately.)

**ḥ** is an aspiration following the vowel, e.g., **aḥ** is like 'uh'.

**ṛ** is a vocalized 'r' pronounced like 'ri' with a rolled 'r'.

**ś** is pronounced 'sh' and **ṣ** is a retroflex 'sh' pronounced with the tongue turned back.

The nasalizations are similar to the Pāli and are presented in various forms (**n, ṅ, ñ, ṇ, m** or **ṃ**), as seems appropriate to approximate the proper sound for an English speaker.

## The Opening Night of the Ten-day Course

| | |
|---|---|
| *Namo tassa bhagavato, arahato,*<br>*sammā-sambuddhassa.* | Homage to him, the blessed one, the worthy<br>conqueror, the fully self-enlightened Buddha. |

### Opening Hindi Chanting

| | |
|---|---|
| *Jaya jaya jaya gurudevajū,*<br>*jaya jaya kripānidhāna;*<br>*dharama ratana aisā diyā,*<br>*huvā parama kalyāṇa.* | My teacher, may you be victorious;<br>Compassionate one, may you be victorious<br>You gave me such a jewel of Dhamma,<br>which has been so beneficial to me. |
| *Aisā cakhāyā dharama rasa,*<br>*biṣayana rasa na lubhāya;*<br>*dharama sāra aisā diyā,*<br>*chilake diye chuḍāya.* | You let me taste Dhamma's nectar,<br>now no sensual pleasure can allure.<br>Such an essence of Dhamma you gave,<br>that the shell [of ignorance] dropped away. |
| *Dharama diyā kaisā sabala,*<br>*paga paga kare sahāya;*<br>*bhaya bhairava sāre miṭe,*<br>*nirbhaya diyā banāya.* | You gave such a powerful Dhamma,<br>which helps and supports me at every step.<br>It has helped to rid me of all fears,<br>and made me absolutely fearless. |
| *Roma roma kirataga huvā,*<br>*ṛṇa na cukāyā jāya;*<br>*jīvūṅ jīvana dharama kā,*<br>*dukhiyana bāṭūṅ dharama sukha,*<br><br>*yahī ucita upāya.* | From every pore such gratitude is pouring<br>I cannot repay the debt.<br>I will live the Dhamma life<br>and distribute its benefit to the suffering people<br>[of the world]:<br>this is the only way [to repay the debt]. |
| *Dharama gaṅga ke tīra para,*<br>*dukhiyāroṅ kī bhīḍa;*<br>*saba ke mana ke dukha miṭe,*<br>*dūra hoya bhava pīḍa.* | On the bank of the Ganges of Dhamma<br>there is a crowd of suffering people;<br>may all be freed from their misery and<br>liberated from the pain of birth and death. |

| | |
|---|---|
| *Guruvara terī ora se,* | O my teacher, on your behalf, |
| *devūṅ dharama ka dāna;* | I give the *dāna* of Dhamma. |
| *jo jo āye tapa karaṇa,* | May all who have come to meditate |
| *ho sabaka kalyāṇa.* | be happy and peaceful. |
| | |
| *Sabake mana jāge dharama,* | May Dhamma arise in everyone's mind. |
| *mukti dukhoṅ se hoya;* | May they be liberated from suffering. |
| *antara kī gāṅtheṅ khule,* | May their innermost mental knots be untied. |
| *mānasa niramala hoya,* | May their minds be purified. |
| *saba ka maṅgala hoya.* | May all be happy and peaceful. |
| | |
| *Ananta pūṇyamayī,* | Source of infinite merit, |
| *ananta guṇamayī,* | of infinite virtues, |
| *buddha kī nirvāṇa-dhātu,* | [is] the Buddha's element of *nibbāna*, |
| *dharama-dhātu, bodhi-dhātu.* | of Dhamma, of enlightenment! |
| *Śīśa para jāge sabhī ke,* | May it arise on the [top of the] head of everyone, |
| *hṛdaya meṅ jāge sabhī ke,* | in the heart of everyone, |
| *aṅga-aṅga jāge sabhī ke.* | in every part of the body of everyone. |
| | |
| *Ananta pūṇyamayī* | Source of infinite merit, |
| *ananta guṇamayī,* | of infinite benefit, |
| *dharama kī nirvāṇa-dhātu,* | [is] the Dhamma's element of *nibbāna*, |
| *jñāna-dhātu, bodhi-dhātu.* | of wisdom, of enlightenment! |
| *Śīśa para jāge sabhī ke,* | May it arise on the [top of the] head of everyone, |
| *hṛdaya meṅ jāge sabhī ke,* | in the heart of everyone, |
| *aṅga-aṅga jāge sabhī ke.* | in every part of the body of everyone. |
| | |
| *Ananta pūṇyamayī* | Source of infinite merit, |
| *ananta guṇamayī,* | of infinite benefit, |
| *saṅgha kī nirvāṇa-dhātu,* | [are] the Sangha's element of *nibbāna*, |
| *dharama-dhātu, bodhi-dhātu.* | of Dhamma, of enlightenment! |
| *Śīśa para jāge sabhī ke,* | May it arise on the [top of the] head of everyone, |
| *hṛdaya meṅ jāge sabhī ke,* | in the heart of everyone, |
| *aṅga-aṅga jāge sabhī ke.* | in every part of the body of everyone. |

## Pāli Formalities

| | |
|---|---|
| **Tisaraṇaṃ-gamanaṃ** | **Going for Triple Refuge** |
| *Buddhaṃ saraṇaṃ gacchāmi.* | I take refuge in the Buddha. |
| *Dhammaṃ saraṇaṃ gacchāmi.* | I take refuge in the Dhamma. |
| *Saṅghaṃ saraṇaṃ gacchāmi.* | I take refuge in the Sangha. |
| | |
| ***Pañca-sīla*** | **The Five Precepts** |
| *Pāṇātipātā veramaṇī sikkhāpadaṃ samādiyāmi.* | I undertake the rule of training to abstain from killing living creatures. |
| *Adinnādānā veramaṇī sikkhāpadaṃ samādiyāmi.* | I undertake the rule of training to abstain from taking what is not given. |
| *Kāmesu micchācārā veramaṇī sikkhāpadaṃ samādiyāmi.* | I undertake the rule of training to abstain from sexual misconduct. |
| *Musā-vādā veramaṇī sikkhāpadaṃ samādiyāmi.* | I undertake the rule of training to abstain from wrong speech. |
| *Surā-meraya-majjapamādaṭṭhānā veramaṇī sikkhāpadaṃ samādiyāmi.* | I undertake the rule of training to abstain from intoxicants, which are the causes of heedlessness. |
| | |
| ***Aṭṭhaṅga-sīla*** | **The Eight Precepts** |
| *Pāṇātipātā veramaṇī sikkhāpadaṃ samādiyāmi.* | I undertake the rule of training to abstain from killing living creatures. |
| *Adinnādānā veramaṇī sikkhāpadaṃ samādiyāmi.* | I undertake the rule of training to abstain from taking what is not given. |
| *Abrahmacariyā veramaṇī sikkhāpadaṃ samādiyāmi.* | I undertake the rule of training to abstain from sexual activity. |
| *Musā-vādā veramaṇī sikkhāpadaṃ samādiyāmi.* | I undertake the rule of training to abstain from wrong speech. |
| *Surā-meraya-majja-pamādaṭṭhānā veramaṇī sikkhāpadaṃ samādiyāmi.* | I undertake the rule of training to abstain from intoxicants, which are the causes of heedlessness. |
| *Vikālabhojanā veramaṇī sikkhāpadaṃ samādiyāmi.* | I undertake the rule of training to abstain from eating at the wrong time. |
| *Nacca-gīta-vādita-visūkadassanā-mālā-gandha-vilepana-dhāraṇa-maṇḍana-vibhūsanaṭṭhānā veramaṇī sikkhāpadaṃ samādiyāmi.* | I undertake the rule of training to abstain from dancing, singing, music, and worldly entertainments; [wearing] garlands, perfumes, cosmetics; jewelry and other bodily adornments. |

*Uccāsayana-mahāsayanā veramaṇi sikkhāpadaṃ samādiyāmi.*

I undertake the rule of training to abstain from using high or luxurious beds.

***Pariccajāmi***

*Imāhaṃ bhante attabhāvaṃ jīvitaṃ bhagavato pariccajāmi.*

*Imāhaṃ bhante attabhāvaṃ jīvitaṃ ācariyassa pariccajāmi.*

**The Surrender**

Sir, I surrender my life completely to the Buddha [for proper guidance and protection].

Sir, I surrender my life completely to my present teacher [for proper guidance and protection].

***Kammaṭṭhāna***

*Nibbānassa sacchikaraṇatthāya me bhante ānāpāna kammaṭṭhānaṃ dehi.*

**The Request of Dhamma**

For the sake of witnessing *nibbāna*, Sir, grant me the meditation object of Anapana.

## Closing Chanting, after Anapana Instructions

### Hindi:

| | |
|---|---|
| *Sādhaka terā ho bhalā,* | O meditator, may you be happy, |
| *ho maṅgala kalyāṇa;* | be peaceful, be liberated; |
| *Sāṅsa sāṅsa ko nirakhate,* | remaining aware of every breath, |
| *dṛḍha ho ānāpāna.* | may your Anapana be firmly rooted. |
| *Beṭī terā ho bhalā,* | O daughter, may you be happy, |
| *ho terā kalyāṇa;* | be peaceful, be liberated; |
| *Sāṅsa sāṅsa para mana ṭike,* | concentrating on every breath, |
| *dṛḍha ho jāye dhyāna* | may your meditation be firmly rooted. |

### Pāli:

| | |
|---|---|
| *Bhavatu sabba maṅgalaṃ. (3x)* | May all beings be happy. |
| *[Sādhu, sādhu, sādhu.]* | [Well said, well said, well said.] |

## The Daily Morning Chanting

*Goenkaji begins each day of the ten-day course with a session of chanting just before breakfast, as the sun is rising. This daily morning chanting session has a basic structure. It begins with Hindi dohas of Goenkaji's own composition, exhorting everyone to awake and listen to words of Dhamma. This is followed by a section of Pāli chanting that is repeated each day with a few variations. Then comes the main sutta of that day, followed by a closing section of Hindi dohas and wishes of welfare for all the students.*

*This chapter gives the basic framework of the morning chanting, along with the daily variations. The main sutta for each day is presented separately in the subsequent chapters.*

### Hindi

| | |
|---|---|
| *1.a) Jāgo logo jagata ke,<br>bītī kālī rāta;<br>huā ujālā dharama kā<br>maṅgala huā prabhāta.* | People of the world, awake!<br>The dark night is over.<br>The light has come of Dhamma,<br>the dawn of happiness. |
| *Āo prāṇī viśva ke,<br>suno Dharama kā jñāna;<br>isa meṅ sukha hai, śānti hai,<br>mukti mokṣa nirvāṇa.* | Come, beings of the universe,<br>listen to the wisdom of the Dhamma.<br>In this lie happiness and peace,<br>freedom, liberation, *nibbāna*. |
| *Yaha to vāṇi buddha kī,<br>śuddha dharama kī jyota;<br>akṣara akṣara meṅ bharā,<br>maṅgala otaparota.* | These are the words of the Buddha,<br>the radiance of pure Dhamma,<br>each syllable of them filled<br>and permeated with happiness. |
| *Buddha-vāṇī mīṭhī ghaṇī,<br>misarī ke se bola;<br>kalyāṇī maṅgalamayī,<br>bharā amṛtarasa ghola.* | Sweet are the words of the Buddha,<br>each phrase like honey,<br>yielding welfare and happiness,<br>suffused with the taste of the deathless. |

## Or (days 8, 9, 10)

| | |
|---|---|
| *1.b) Jāgo logo jagata ke,*<br>*bītī kālī rāta;*<br>*huā ujālā dharama kā,*<br>*maṅgala huā prabhāta.* | People of the world, awake!<br>The dark night is over.<br>The light has come of Dhamma,<br>the dawn of happiness. |
| *Āo prāṇī viśva ke,*<br>*caleṅ dharama ke pantha;*<br>*dharama pantha hī śānti patha,*<br>*dharama pantha sukha pantha.* | Come, beings of the universe,<br>let us walk the path of Dhamma.<br>The path of Dhamma is the path of peace,<br>the path of Dhamma is the path of happiness. |
| *Ādi māṅhi kalyāṇa hai,*<br>*madhya māṅhi kalyāṇa;*<br>*anta māṅhi kalyāṇa hai,*<br>*kadama kadama kalyāṇa.* | Beneficial in the beginning,<br>beneficial in the middle,<br>beneficial at the end—<br>every step is beneficial. |
| *Śīla māṅhi kalyāṇa hai,*<br>*hai samādhi kalyāṇa;*<br>*prajñā to kalyāṇa hai,*<br>*pragaṭe pada nirvāṇa.* | There is benefit in moral conduct,<br>benefit in controlling the mind,<br>benefit in wisdom,<br>leading to *nibbāna*. |
| *Kitane dina bhaṭakata phire,*<br>*andhī galiṅyoṇ māṅhi!*<br>*Aba to pāyā rāja-patha, vāpasa*<br>*muḍanā nāṅhi.*<br>*Aba to pāyā vimala patha,*<br>*pīche haṭanā nāṅhi.* | How many days did we keep wandering<br>in blind alleys!<br>Now that we have found the royal road,<br>we will never look back again.<br>Now that we have found the pure path,<br>we will never turn back. |

## Pāli

| | |
|---|---|
| *2.a)* ***Deva-āhvānasuttaṃ***<br>*Samantā cakkavāḷesu,*<br>*atrāgacchantu devatā; (3x)*<br>*saddhammaṃ munirājassa,*<br>*suṇantu sagga-mokkhadaṃ.*<br>*Dhammassavaṇakālo ayaṃ,*<br>*bhadantā' (3x)* | **Address to the Devas**<br>From throughout the world systems<br>assemble here, oh devas,<br>to listen to the pure Dhamma of the king of sages, leading to heaven and liberation.<br>It is now time for listening to the Dhamma , respected ones. |

## Or (days 2, 4, 6, 8, 9)

| | |
|---|---|
| *2.b) Ye santā santa-cittā,*<br>*tisaraṇa-saraṇā,*<br>*ettha lokantare vā;* | Those peaceful ones of peaceful mind,<br>whose refuge is the Triple Gem<br>in this world or beyond; |
| *bhummābhummā ca devā,*<br>*guṇa-gaṇa-gahaṇā,*<br>*byāvaṭā sabbakālaṃ;* | devas dwelling on earth or elsewhere,<br>who are unceasingly acquiring<br>numerous merits; |
| *ete āyantu devā, (3x)*<br>*vara-kanaka-maye,*<br>*Merurāje vasanto;* | may those devas come<br>who dwell on royal Meru,<br>the glorious golden mountain; |
| *santo santosa-hetuṃ,*<br>*munivara-vacanaṃ,*<br>*sotumaggaṃ samaggaṃ. (3x)* | [may they come] for peace and contentment,<br>and together may they listen<br>to the excellent words of the Buddha. |
| *3.) Namo tassa bhagavato arahato*<br>*sammā-sambuddhassa. (3x)* | Homage to him, the blessed one, the worthy<br>conqueror, the fully self-enlightened Buddha. |
| *4.) Buddhaṃ saraṇaṃ gacchāmi;*<br>*dhammaṃ saraṇaṃ gacchāmi;*<br>*saṅghaṃ saraṇaṃ gacchāmi.* | I take refuge in the Buddha,<br>I take refuge in the Dhamma,<br>I take refuge in the Sangha. |
| *5.) Imāya*<br>*dhammānudhammapaṭipattiyā,*<br>*buddhaṃ pūjemi;*<br>*dhammaṃ pūjemi;*<br>*saṅghaṃ pūjemi.* | By walking on the path of Dhamma<br>from the first step to the final goal,<br>I pay respects to the Buddha;<br>I pay respects to the Dhamma;<br>I pay respects to the Sangha. |
| *6.) Ye ca Buddhā atītā ca,*<br>*ye ca Buddhā anāgatā;*<br>*paccuppannā ca ye Buddhā,*<br>*ahaṃ vandāmi sabbadā.* | To the Buddhas of the past,<br>to the Buddhas yet to come,<br>to the Buddhas of the present,<br>always I pay respects. |

| | |
|---|---|
| *Ye ca Dhammā atītā ca,*<br>*ye ca Dhammā anāgatā;*<br>*paccuppannā ca ye Dhammā,*<br>*ahaṃ vandāmi sabbadā.* | To the Dhammas of the past,<br>to the Dhammas yet to come,<br>to the Dhammas of the present,<br>always I pay respects. |
| *Ye ca Saṅghā atītā ca,*<br>*ye ca Saṅghā anāgatā;*<br>*paccuppannā ca ye Saṅghā,*<br>*ahaṃ vandāmi sabbadā.* | To the Sanghas of the past,<br>to the Sanghas yet to come,<br>to the Sanghas of the present,<br>always I pay respects. |
| 7.) *Natthi me saraṇaṃ aññaṃ,*<br>*Buddho me saraṇaṃ varaṃ;*<br>*etena sacca-vajjena,*<br>*jayassu jaya-maṅgalaṃ.* | No other refuge have I,<br>the Buddha is my supreme refuge.<br>By this true utterance<br>may there be victory and happiness. |
| *Natthi me saraṇaṃ aññaṃ,*<br>*Dhammo me saraṇaṃ varaṃ;*<br>*etena sacca-vajjena,*<br>*bhavatu te jaya-maṅgalaṃ.* | No other refuge have I,<br>the Dhamma is my supreme refuge.<br>By this true utterance<br>may you have victory and happiness. |
| *Natthi me saraṇaṃ aññaṃ,*<br>*Saṅgho me saraṇaṃ varaṃ;*<br>*etena sacca-vajjena,*<br>*bhavatu sabba-maṅgalaṃ.* | No other refuge have I,<br>the Sangha is my supreme refuge.<br>By this true utterance<br>may all beings be happy. |

## Tiratana Vandanā

| | |
|---|---|
| 8.) *Iti'pi so bhagavā*<br>*arahaṃ,*<br>*sammā-sambuddho,*<br>*vijjācaraṇa-sampanno,*<br>*sugato,*<br>*lokavidū,*<br>*anuttaro purisa-damma-sārathī,*<br>*satthā deva-manussānaṃ,*<br>*Buddho Bhagavā 'ti.* | Such truly is he: freed from impurities,<br>having destroyed all mental defilements,<br>fully enlightened by his own efforts,<br>perfect in theory and in practice,<br>having reached the final goal,<br>knower of the entire universe,<br>incomparable trainer of men,<br>teacher of gods and humans,<br>the Buddha, the Blessed One. |

| | |
|---|---|
| 9.) *Svākkhāto Bhagavatā Dhammo,* | Clearly expounded is the teaching of the Blessed One, |
| *sandiṭṭhiko,* | to be seen for oneself, |
| *akāliko,* | giving results here and now, |
| *ehi-passiko,* | inviting one to come and see, |
| *opaneyyiko,* | leading straight to the goal, |
| *paccattaṃ veditabbo viññūhī' ti.* | capable of being realized by any intelligent person. |
| 10.) *Suppaṭipanno Bhagavato sāvaka-saṅgho;* | Those who have practiced well form the order of disciples of the Blessed One; |
| *ujuppaṭipanno Bhagavato sāvaka-saṅgho;* | those who have practiced uprightly form the order of disciples of the Blessed One; |
| *ñāyappaṭipanno Bhagavato sāvaka saṅgho;* | those who have practiced wisely form the order of disciples of the Blessed One; |
| *sāmīcippaṭipanno Bhagavato sāvaka-saṅgho;* | those who have practiced properly form the order of disciples of the Blessed One; |
| *yadidaṃ cattāri purisa-yugāni,* | that is, the four pairs of persons, |
| *aṭṭha-purisa-puggalā,* | the eight kinds of individuals — |
| *esa Bhagavato sāvaka-saṅgho;* | these form the order of disciples of the Blessed One: |
| *āhuneyyo, pāhuneyyo,* | worthy of gifts, of hospitality, |
| *dakkhiṇeyyo, añjali-karaṇīyo,* | of offerings, of reverent salutation, |
| *anuttaraṃ puññakkhettaṃ lokassā'ti.* | an incomparable field of merit for the world. |

**The Pāli *sutta* for each day occurs at this point**

## Post-Pāli Sutta

*This stanza, from Ratana Sutta, occurs each day at the end of the sutta for that day. It signals the end of the Pāli section of the morning chanting and is followed by the Hindi concluding verses.*

| | |
|---|---|
| *Yānīdha bhūtāni samāgatāni,* | Whatever beings are here assembled, |
| *bhummāni vā yānī'va antalikkhe;* | whether terrestrial or celestial, |
| *tathāgataṃ devamanussapūjitaṃ,* | the Tathāgata is revered by gods and men; |
| *buddhaṃ namassāma suvatthi hotu;* | we pay respects to the Buddha; [by the utterance of this truth] may there be happiness; |
| *dhammaṃ namassāma suvatthi hotu;* | we pay respects to the Dhamma; [by the utterance of this truth] may there be happiness; |
| *saṅghaṃ namassāma suvatthi hotu.* | we pay respects to the Sangha; [by the utterance of this truth] may there be happiness. |

## Hindi

### Day 1

| | |
|---|---|
| *Namana karūṅ gurudeva ko,* | I pay homage to my revered teacher, |
| *caraṇana śīśa navāya;* | bowing my head at his feet; |
| *dharama ratana aisā diyā,* | He gave me such a jewel of Dhamma |
| *pāpa samīpa na āya.* | that evil cannot approach. |
| | |
| *Aisā cakhāyā dharama rasa,* | He let me taste Dhamma's nectar, |
| *biṣayana rasa na lubhāya;* | now no sensual pleasure can allure. |
| *dharama sāra aisā diyā,* | Such an essence of Dhamma he gave, |
| *chilake diye chuḍāya.* | that the shell [of ignorance] dropped away. |
| | |
| *Roma roma kirataga huā,* | From every pore such gratitude is pouring |
| *ṛṇa na cukāyā jāya;* | I cannot repay the debt. |
| *jīūṅ jīvana dharama kā,* | I will live the Dhamma life |
| *dukhiyana kī sevā karūṅ,* | and serve the suffering people [of the world], |
| *yahī ucita upāya.* | this is the only way [to repay the debt]. |

| | |
|---|---|
| *Isa sevā ke puṇya se,*<br>*bhalā sabhī kā hoya;*<br>*jo jo āye tapa karaṇa,*<br>*sabakā maṅgala hoya.* | By the merits of this service,<br>may all beings be happy!<br>All those who have come to meditate,<br>May they all be happy! |
| *Bhavatu sabba maṅgalaṃ.* | May all beings be happy. |
| *Sabakā maṅgala, sabakā maṅgala,*<br>*sabakā maṅgala hoya re.*<br>*Terā maṅgala, terā maṅgala,*<br>*terā maṅgala hoya re.* | May all be happy, may all be happy,<br>may all be happy!<br>May you be happy, may you be happy,<br>may you be happy! |
| *Jo jo āye tapa karane ko, (2x)*<br>*saba ke dukhaḍe dūra hoṅ. (2x)*<br>*Janama janama ke bandhana ṭūṭeṅ,*<br><br>*antaratama kī gāṅṭheṅ ṭūṭeṅ;*<br><br>*mānasa niramala hoya re.* | All those who have come to meditate,<br>may they be free from anguish.<br>May they be liberated from the bondage of the cycle of existence,<br>May the innermost knots in their minds be untied.<br>May their minds be purified. |
| *Sabakā maṅgala, sabakā maṅgala,*<br>*sabakā maṅgala hoya re.*<br>*Terā maṅgala, terā maṅgala,*<br>*terā maṅgala hoya re.*<br>*Jana jana maṅgala,*<br>*jana jana maṅgala,*<br>*jana jana sukhiyā hoya re.* | May all be happy, may all be happy,<br>may all be happy!<br>May you be happy, may you be happy,<br>may you be happy!<br>May all beings be happy,<br>may all beings be happy,<br>may all beings be peaceful! |

## Day 2

*The first three dohas are repeated with occasional variants and the 'Sabakā maṅgala' closing is similar with some variation each day. Only the variants for each day follow:*

| | |
|---|---|
| *Namana karūṅ gurudeva ko . . .*<br>*. . . yahī ucita upāya.* | I pay homage to my revered teacher . . .<br>. . . this is the only way [to repay the debt]. |
| *Isa sevā ke puṇya se,*<br>*bhalā sabhī kā hoya;*<br>*sabake mana jāge dharama,*<br>*sabakā maṅgala hoya.* | By the merits of this service,<br>may all be happy!<br>May Dhamma arise in the minds of all,<br>may all be happy. |
| *Bhavatu sabba maṅgalaṃ. (3x)* | May all beings be happy. |
| *Sabakā maṅgala, . . .* | May all be happy, . . . |
| *Isa dharatī ke jitane prāṇī, (2x)*<br>*sabake dukhaḍe dūra hoṅ. (2x)*<br>*Janama janama ke bandhana ṭūṭeṅ,*<br><br>*antaratama kī gāṅṭheṅ ṭūṭeṅ;*<br>*mānasa niramala hoya re.* | All the beings on this earth,<br>may they be free from suffering.<br>May they be liberated from the bondage of [the cycle of] existence,<br>May their innermost mental knots be untied.<br>May their minds be purified. |
| *Sabakā maṅgala, . . .*<br>*Terā maṅgala, . . .*<br>*Jana jana maṅgala, . . .* | May all be happy, . . .<br>May you be happy, . . .<br>May all beings be happy, . . . |

## Day 3

| | |
|---|---|
| *Namana karūṅ gurudeva ko . . .*<br>*. . . yahī ucita upāya.* | I pay homage to my revered teacher . . .<br>. . . this is the only way [to repay the debt]. |
| *Isa sevā ke puṇya se,*<br>*bhalā sabhī kā hoya;*<br>*Sabake mana jāge dharama,*<br>*mukti dukhoṅ se hoya,*<br>*sabakā maṅgala hoya.* | By the merits of this service,<br>may all beings be happy!<br>May Dhamma arise in the minds of all,<br>may they be free from suffering!<br>May all be happy! |

| | |
|---|---|
| *Bhavatu sabba maṅgalaṃ. (3x)* | May all beings be happy. |
| | |
| *Sabakā maṅgala, . . .* | May all be happy, . . . |
| *Terā maṅgala, . . .* | May you be happy, . . . |
| | |
| *Dṛśya aura adṛśya,* | Visible or invisible, |
| *sabhī jīvoṅ kā maṅgala hoya re. (2x)* | may all beings be happy. |
| *Nirabhaya hoṅ nirabaira bane saba,(2x)* | May all be free from fear and animosity, |
| *nirabhaya hoṅ nirabaira bane saba,* | may all be free from fear and animosity, |
| *sabhī nirāmaya hoṅya re.* | may all be free from illness. |
| | |
| *Sabakā maṅgala, . . .* | May all be happy, . . . |
| *Terā maṅgala, . . .* | May you be happy, . . . |
| *Jana jana maṅgala, . . .* | May all beings be happy, . . . |

## Day 4

| | |
|---|---|
| *Namana karūṅ gurudeva ko,* | I pay homage to my revered teacher, |
| *sādara śīśa navāya;* | respectfully bowing my head. |
| *dharama ratana aisā diyā,* | He gave me such a jewel of Dhamma he gave |
| *pāpa panapa nahīṅ pāya.* | that evil cannot thrive within me. |
| | |
| *Aisā cakhāyā dharama rasa . . .* | He let me taste Dhamma's nectar, . . . |
| *. . . yahī ucita upāya.* | . . . this is the only way [to repay the debt]. |
| | |
| *Āja dharama kā divasa hai,* | Today is the day of Dhamma, |
| *deūṅ dharama kā dāna;* | I give the gift of Dhamma. |
| *jo āye tapane yahāṅ,* | All those who have come to meditate here |
| *ho sabakā kalyāṇa,* | may they all be happy, |
| *ho sabakā kalyāṇa.* | may they all be happy. |
| | |
| *Bhavatu sabba maṅgalaṃ. (3x)* | May all beings be happy. |
| | |
| *Sabakā maṅgala, . . .* | May all be happy, . . . |
| | |
| *Jo jo āye tapa karane ko, (2x)* | All those who have come to meditate, |
| *sabake dukhaḍe dūra hoṅ, (2x)* | may they be free from anguish. |
| *Sabake mana prajñā jaga jāye, (2x)* | May wisdom arise in the minds of all, |
| *antasa niramala hoya re. (2x)* | may their minds be totally purified. |

| | |
|---|---|
| *Sabakā maṅgala, . . .* | May all be happy, . . . |
| *Terā maṅgala, . . .* | May you be happy, . . . |
| *Jana jana maṅgala, . . .* | May all beings be happy, . . . |

## Day 5

| | |
|---|---|
| *Namana karūṅ gurudeva ko,* | I pay homage to my revered teacher, |
| *savinaya śīśa navāya;* | humbly bowing my head. |
| *dharama ratana aisā diyā,* | He gave me such a jewel of Dhamma |
| *pāpa nikaṭa nahīṅ āya.* | that evil cannot approach. |
| | |
| *Aisā cakhāyā dharama rasa . . .* | He let me taste Dhamma's nectar, . . . |
| *. . . yahī ucita upāya.* | . . . this is the only way [to repay the debt]. |
| | |
| *Isa sevā ke puṇya se,* | By the merits of this service, |
| *dharama ujāgara hoya;* | may Dhamma spread. |
| *kaṭe andherā pāpa kā,* | May the darkness of evil be eradicated, |
| *jana mana harakhita hoya,* | may the minds of all be gladdened, |
| *sabakā maṅgala hoya.* | may all be happy. |
| | |
| *Bhavatu sabba maṅgalaṃ. (3x)* | May all beings be happy. |
| | |
| *Sabakā maṅgala, . . .* | May all be happy, . . . |
| | |
| *Śuddha dharama dharatī para jāge,* | May pure Dhamma arise on this earth, |
| *śuddha dharama dharatī para jāge,* | may pure Dhamma arise on this earth, |
| *pāpa parājita hoya re,* | may evil be defeated, |
| *pāpa tirohita hoya re;* | may evil be dispelled. |
| *Jana mana ke dukhaḍe miṭa jāyeṅ, (2x)* | May the anguish in the minds of all be extinguished, |
| *jana jana maṅgala hoya re.* | may all be happy. |
| | |
| *Sabakā maṅgala, . . .* | May all be happy, . . . |
| *Terā maṅgala, . . .* | May you be happy, . . . |
| *Jana jana maṅgala, . . .* | May all beings be happy, . . . |

## Day 6

| | |
|---|---|
| *Namana karūṅ gurudeva ko,* | I pay homage to my revered teacher, |
| *caraṇana śīśa navāya;* | bowing my head at his feet. |
| *dharama ratana aisā diyā,* | He gave me such a jewel of Dhamma |
| *pāpa panapa nahīṅ pāya.* | that evil cannot thrive within me. |
| *Aisā cakhāyā dharama rasa . . .* | He let me taste Dhamma's nectar, . . . |
| *. . . yahī ucita upāya.* | . . . this is the only way [to repay the debt]. |
| *Isa sevā ke puṇya se,* | By the merits of this service, |
| *dharama ujāgara hoya;* | may Dhamma spread. |
| *kaṭe andherā pāpa kā,* | May the darkness of evil be eradicated, |
| *jana jana hita-sukha hoya, (2x)* | may all beings be happy and prosperous, |
| *jana jana maṅgala hoya.* | may all beings be happy. |
| *Bhavatu sabba maṅgalaṃ. (3x)* | May all beings be happy. |
| *Sabakā maṅgala, . . .* | May all be happy, . . . |
| *Isa dharatī ke taru-tṛṇa meṅ,* | May every tree, every blade of grass, |
| *kaṇa-kaṇa meṅ* | and every particle of this earth |
| *dharama samā jāye. (2x)* | be suffused with Dhamma. |
| *Jo bhī tape isa tapobhūmi para, (2x)* | May all who meditate on this Dhamma land, |
| *mukta dukhoṅ se ho jāye. (2x)* | be liberated from all suffering, (2x) |
| *Sabakā maṅgala, . . .* | May all be happy, . . . |
| *Terā maṅgala, . . .* | May you be happy, . . . |
| *Jana jana maṅgala, . . .* | May all beings be happy, . . . |

## Day 7

| | |
|---|---|
| *Namana karūṅ gurudeva ko,* | I pay homage to my revered teacher, |
| *caraṇana śīśa navāya;* | bowing my head at his feet. |
| *dharama ratana aisā diyā,* | He gave me such a jewel of Dhamma |
| *pāpa nikaṭa nahīṅ āya.* | that evil cannot approach. |
| *Aisā cakhāyā dharama rasa . . .* | He let me taste Dhamma's nectar, . . . |
| *. . . yahī ucita upāya.* | . . . this is the only way [to repay the debt]. |

| | |
|---|---|
| *Isa sevā ke puṇya se,* | By the merits of this service, |
| *sukhī hoṅya saba loga;* | may all people be happy. |
| *sabake mana jāge dharama,* | May Dhamma arise in the minds of all, |
| *dūra hoya bhava roga.* | may all be freed from the cycle of existence. |
| | |
| *Dukhiyāre dukhamukta hoṅ,* | May the suffering be freed from suffering, |
| *bhaya tyāgeṅ bhayabhīta;* | may the fearful be freed from fear, |
| *baira choḍa kara loga saba,* | Renouncing enmity, may all beings |
| *kareṅ paraspara prīta.* | have affection for one another. |
| | |
| *Bhavatu sabba maṅgalaṃ. (3x)* | May all beings be happy. |
| | |
| *Sabakā maṅgala, . . .* | May all be happy, . . . |
| | |
| *Isa dharatī ke jitane prāṇī,* | May all the beings on this earth, |
| *tapobhūmi ke jitane tāpasa,* | may all the meditators on this Dhamma land, |
| *maṅgala se bharapūra hoṅ. (2x)* | be filled with happiness. |
| *Rāga dveṣa sabake miṭa jāyeṅ, (2x)* | May their craving and aversion be eradicated, |
| *roga śoka saba dūra hoṅ. (2x)* | may they be free of disease and sorrows. |
| | |
| *Sabakā maṅgala, . . .* | May all be happy, . . . |
| *Terā maṅgala, . . .* | May you be happy, . . . |
| *Jana jana maṅgala, . . . hoya re.* | May all beings be happy, . . . |

## Day 8

| | |
|---|---|
| *Namana karūṅ gurudeva ko,* | I pay homage to my revered teacher, |
| *sādara śīśa navāya;* | respectfully bowing my head. |
| *dharama ratana aisā diyā,* | Such a jewel of Dhamma he gave |
| *pāpa upaja nahīṅ pāya.* | that evil cannot arise in me. |
| | |
| *Aisā cakhāyā dharama rasa . . .* | He let me taste Dhamma's nectar, . . . |
| *. . . yahī ucita upāya.* | . . . this is the only way [to repay the debt]. |
| | |
| *Isa sevā ke puṇya se,* | By the merits of this service, |
| *dharama ujāgara hoya;* | may the light of Dhamma spread. |
| *kaṭe andherā pāpa kā,* | May the darkness of evil be eradicated, |
| *jana mana harakhita hoya.* | may the minds of all be gladdened. |

| | |
|---|---|
| *Barase barakhā samaya para,*<br>*dūra rahe duṣkāla;*<br>*śāsāna hove dharama kā, (3x)*<br>*loga hoṅya khuśahāla.*<br>*Sukha vyāpe isa jagata meṅ,*<br>*dukhiyā rahe na koya;*<br>*sabake mana jāge dharama,*<br>*sabakā maṅgala hoya. (2x)* | May it rain at the proper time,<br>may there be no famine.<br>May the government be righteous,<br>may the people be prosperous.<br>May happiness pervade the world,<br>may no one be unhappy.<br>May Dhamma arise in the minds of all,<br>may all be happy. |
| *Bhavatu sabba maṅgalaṃ. (3x)* | May all beings be happy. |
| *Sabakā maṅgala, . . .* | May all be happy, . . . |
| *Isa dharatī ke taru-tṛṇa meṅ,*<br>*kaṇa-kaṇa meṅ*<br>*dharama samā jāye. (2x)* | May every tree, every blade of grass,<br>and every particle of this earth<br>be permeated with Dhamma. |
| *Jo bhī tape isa tapobhūmi para, (2x)*<br>*mukta dukhoṅ se ho jāye. (2x)* | May all who meditate on this Dhamma land<br>be liberated from all suffering. |
| *Sabakā maṅgala, . . .*<br>*Terā maṅgala, . . .*<br>*Jana jana maṅgala, . . . hoya re.* | May all be happy, . . .<br>May you be happy, . . .<br>May all beings be happy, . . . |

## Day 9

| | |
|---|---|
| *Namana karūṅ gurudeva ko,*<br>*caraṇana śīśa navāya;*<br>*dharama ratana aisā diyā,*<br>*pāpa ukhaḍatā jāya.* | I pay homage to my revered teacher,<br>bowing my head at his feet.<br>he gave me such a jewel of Dhamma<br>that evil within me gets uprooted. |
| *Aisā cakhāyā dharama rasa . . .*<br>*. . . yahī ucita upāya.* | He let me taste Dhamma's nectar, . . .<br>. . . this is the only way [to repay the debt]. |
| *Isa sevā ke puṇya se,*<br>*bhalā sabhī kā hoya;*<br>*sabake mana jāge dharama,*<br>*mukti dukhoṅ se hoya.* | By the merits of this service,<br>may all be happy.<br>May Dhamma arise in the minds of all<br>and liberate them from suffering. |

| | |
|---|---|
| *Dharamavihārī puruṣa hoṅ,* | May every man live a life of Dhamma, |
| *dharamacāriṇī nāra;* | may every woman live a life of Dhamma, |
| *dharamavanta santāna hoṅ,* | may their children live a life of Dhamma, |
| *sukhī rahe parivāra,* | may each family be happy, |
| *sukhī rahe sansāra.* | may household life be happy. |
| | |
| *Bhavatu sabba maṅgalaṃ. (3x)* | May all beings be happy. |
| | |
| *Sabakā maṅgala, . . .* | May all be happy, . . . |
| | |
| *Śuddha dharama ghara ghara meṅ jāge; (2x)* | May pure Dhamma arise in every household, |
| *ghara ghara śānti samāya re. (2x)* | may there be peace in every home, |
| *nara nārī hoṅ dharamavihārī,* | may every man and woman live a life of Dhamma, |
| *saba nara nārī dharamavihārī;* | may all men and women live a life of Dhamma, |
| *ghara ghara maṅgala chāya re. (2x)* | may every household be filled with happiness. |
| | |
| *Sabakā maṅgala, . . .* | May all be happy, . . . |
| *Terā maṅgala, . . .* | May you be happy, . . . |
| *Jana jana maṅgala, . . .* | May all beings be happy, . . . |

## Day 10

*[These verses are before Mettā Bhāvanā on day ten. On the first nine days the first two verses follow the Pāli sutta.]*

| | |
|---|---|
| *Namana karūṅ gurudeva ko,* | I pay homage to my revered teacher, |
| *caraṇana śīśa navāya;* | bowing my head at his feet. |
| *dharama ratana aisā diyā,* | He gave me such a jewel of Dhamma |
| *pāpa upaja nahīṅ pāya.* | that evil cannot arise in me. |
| | |
| *Aisā cakhāyā dharama rasa . . .* | He let me taste Dhamma's nectar, . . . |
| *. . . yahī ucita upāya.* | . . . this is the only way [to repay the debt]. |
| | |
| *Isa dukhiyāre jagata meṅ,* | In this sorrowful world, |
| *sukhiyā dikhe na koya;* | I do not see any happy person. |
| *śuddha dharama phira se jage,* | May the pure Dhamma arise again, |
| *phira se maṅgala hoya.* | may there be happiness again. |
| *Dasoṅ diśāoṅ ke sabhī prāṇī* | May all the beings of the ten directions |

| | |
|---|---|
| *sukhiyā hoṅya;* | be happy; |
| *nirabhaya hoṅ, nirabaira hoṅ,* | may they be free from fear, free from enmity, |
| *sabhī nirāmaya hoṅya.* | may they all be free from disease. |
| *Sabakā maṅgala hoya.* | May all be happy. |

*[after Mettā Bhāvanā]*

| | |
|---|---|
| *Bhavatu sabba maṅgalaṃ. (3x)* | May all beings be happy. |
| *Phira se jāge dharama jagata meṅ,* | May Dhamma arise again in the world, |
| *phira se hove jaga kalyāṇa;* | may there be happiness again in the world; |
| *jāge jāge dharama jagata meṅ,* | may Dhamma arise in the world, |
| *hove hove jana kalyāṇa. (2x)* | may there be happiness in the world. |
| *Rāga dveṣa aura moha dūra hoṅ,* | May craving, aversion and ignorance be dispelled, |
| *jāge śīla samādhi jñāna. (2x)* | may morality, concentration and wisdom arise. |
| *Jana mana ke dukhaḍe miṭa jāyeṅ,* | May the anguish in the minds of people end, |
| *phira se jāga uṭhe musakāna; (2x)* | may their smiles be restored again. |
| *Phira se jāge dharama jagata meṅ,* | May Dhamma arise again in the world, |
| *phira se hove jaga kalyāṇa.* | may there be happiness again in the world. |
| *Jāge jāge dharama kī vāṇī,* | May the words of Dhamma arise, |
| *maṅgala mūla mahā kalyāṇī; (2x)* | root of all happiness and well-being; |
| *jāge jāge dharama kī vāṇī.* | may the words of Dhamma arise. |
| *Jāge buddha sadṛśa koī jñānī,* | May a wise one like the Buddha arise again, |
| *hoṅya sukhī saba jaga ke prāṇī. (2x)* | may all beings in the world be happy. (2x) |
| *Jāge jāge dharama kī vāṇī,* | May the words of Dhamma arise, |
| *maṅgala mūla mahā kalyāṇī; (2x)* | root of all happiness and well-being. |
| *Jāge jāge dharama kī vāṇī,* | May the words of Dhamma arise, |
| *jāge buddha sadṛśa koī jñānī,* | may a wise one like the Buddha arise again, |
| *hoṅya sukhī saba jaga ke prāṇī.* | may all beings in the world be happy. |

## Day 11

*Before the final discourse, on the closing morning of the course, the opening Hindi verses and the initial Pāli verses that are chanted daily are omitted. The chanting begins directly with Namo tassa . . . (see pages 7 - 9, numbers 3 - 5). The following Hindi verses then conclude the morning chanting, leading up to the discourse.*

| | |
|---|---|
| *Namaskāra hai buddha ko,*<br>*kaise karuṇāgāra;*<br>*dukkha miṭāvana patha diyā,*<br>*sukhi karana sansāra.* | Homage to the Buddha,<br>such a treasure house of compassion;<br>he showed us the path to eradicate suffering,<br>bringing happiness to the world. |
| *Namaskāra hai dharama ko,*<br>*kaisā pāvana pantha;*<br>*jo bhi cale isa pantha para,*<br>*vahī bana gaye santa.* | Homage to the Dhamma,<br>such a pure path;<br>whoever walks on this path<br>becomes a saintly person. |
| *Namaskāra hai saṅgha ko,*<br>*kaise śrāvaka santa;*<br>*dharama dhāra ujale huve,*<br>*nirmala huve bhadanta* | Homage to the Sangha,<br>such a noble assembly of disciples;<br>practicing Dhamma, these saintly ones<br>have become radiant and pure. |
| *Namaskāra jananī janaka,*<br>*hai upakāra ananta;*<br>*namaskāra arihanta saba,*<br>*namaskāra saba santa.* | Homage to mother and father,<br>towards whom my debt of gratitude is infinite,<br>homage to all the *arahants*,<br>homage to all the saintly people. |
| *Namasakāra gurudeva ko,*<br>*kaise santa sujāna;*<br>*kitane karuṇā citta se,*<br>*diya dharama kā dāna* | Homage to my teacher,<br>so saintly and wise;<br>with a mind overflowing with compassion,<br>he gave the gift of Dhamma. |
| *Aisā cakhāyā dharama rasa . . .*<br>*. . . yahī eka upāya.* | He let me taste Dhamma's nectar, . . .<br>. . . this is the only way [to repay the debt]. |

| | |
|---|---|
| *Isa sevā ke puṇya se,* | By the merits of this service, |
| *dharama ujāgara hoya;* | may the light of Dhamma spread again. |
| *Jana jana kā hita sukha sadhe,* | May all beings be happy and prosperous, |
| *Jana jana maṅgala hoya,* | may all beings be happy, |
| *saba kā maṅgala hoya.* | may all be happy! |
| *Bhavatu sabba maṅgalaṃ. (3x)* | May all Beings be happy. |

*The closing discourse follows.* *For the final mettā chanting please see pages 74-75.*

## Day One—Āṭānāṭiya Sutta

*This paritta text, composed in post-canonical times in Myanmar, is based on a discourse of the same name found in the Dīgha-nikāya III. 9, except the last verse, which is taken from Dhammapada VIII. 10 (109). The title refers to the town of Āṭānāṭa, where the sutta was first recited. The discourse names the seven most recent Buddhas to have arisen, the last being Siddhattha Gotama.*

| Āṭānāṭiya Sutta | Āṭānāṭiya Discourse |
|---|---|
| *Appasannehi nāthassa,*<br>*sāsane sādhusammate;*<br>*amanussehi caṇḍehi,*<br>*sadā kibbisakāribhi.* | In order that those lacking faith in the Lord's<br>revered teaching,<br>wrathful non-humans<br>ever working evil, |
| *Parisānaṃ catassannaṃ,*<br>*ahiṃsāya ca guttiyā;*<br>*yaṃ desesi Mahāvīro,*<br>*parittaṃ taṃ bhaṇāmahe.* | may protect rather than harm<br>the four assemblies,[1]<br>let us recite this protective verse<br>taught by the Buddha. |
| *Vipassissa ca namatthu,*<br>*cakkhumantassa sirīmato;*<br>*Sikhissapi ca namatthu,*<br>*sabbabhūtānukampino.* | Homage to Vipassī,<br>the glorious one with the eye of wisdom;<br>homage to Sikhī,<br>compassionate to all beings. |
| *Vessabhussa ca namatthu,*<br>*nhātakassa tapassino;*<br>*namatthu Kakusandhassa,*<br>*Mārasenappamaddino.* | Homage to Vessabhū,<br>cleansed of impurities, ardent in meditation;<br>homage to Kakusandha,<br>vanquisher of Māra's army. |
| *Koṇāgamanassa namatthu,*<br>*brāhmaṇassa vusīmato;*<br>*Kassapassa ca namatthu,*<br>*vippamuttassa sabbadhi.* | Homage to Koṇāgamana,<br>of pure life, the perfected one;<br>homage to Kassapa,<br>liberated in every respect. |

| | |
|---|---|
| *Aṅgīrasassa namatthu,* | Homage to the Radiant One [Gotama], |
| *Sakyaputtassa sirīmato;* | the glorious son of the Sakyas, |
| *yo imaṃ dhammaṃ desesi,* | who taught this Dhamma, |
| *sabbadukkhāpanūdanaṃ.* | which dispells all suffering. |
| | |
| *Ye cāpi nibbutā loke,* | They have extinguished [craving toward] the world |
| *yathābhūtaṃ vipassisuṃ;* | and gained insight into reality as it is, |
| *te janā apisuṇātha,* | those persons who utter no evil, |
| *mahantā vītasāradā.* | mighty and experienced. |
| | |
| *Hitaṃ devamanussānaṃ,* | Benefactor of *devas* and humans, |
| *yaṃ namassanti Gotamaṃ;* | revered is Gotama; |
| *vijjācaraṇa-sampannaṃ,* | accomplished in knowledge and conduct, |
| *mahantaṃ vītasāradaṃ.* | mighty and experienced. |
| | |
| *Ete caññe ca sambuddhā,* | These and other fully Enlightened Ones, |
| *anekasata-koṭiyo;* | numbering many hundreds of millions, |
| *sabbe Buddhā samasamā,* | are all alike Buddhas, |
| *sabbe Buddhā mahiddhikā.* | all Buddhas of great power. |
| | |
| *Sabbe dasabalūpetā,* | All are endowed with the ten strengths[2] |
| *vesārajjehupāgatā;* | and have perfect confidence;[3] |
| *sabbe te paṭijānanti,* | everyone acknowledged them |
| *āsabhaṭṭhānamuttamaṃ.* | as unsurpassed leaders. |
| | |
| *Sīhanādaṃ nadantete,* | Like the sound of the lion's roar |
| *parisāsu visāradā;* | is these wise ones' [speech] in assemblies; |
| *brahmacakkaṃ pavattenti,* | they start the Noble Wheel of Dhamma turning |
| *loke appaṭivattiyaṃ.* | in the world, whose movement cannot be reversed. |
| | |
| *Upetā buddhadhammehi,* | These leaders are endowed |
| *aṭṭhārasahi nāyakā;* | with the eighteen virtues of a Buddha,[4] |

| | |
|---|---|
| *battiṃsa-lakkhaṇūpetā,* | and bear the thirty-two major marks |
| *sītānubyañjanā dharā.* | and eighty minor signs [of a Buddha].[5] |
| | |
| *Byāmappabhāya suppabhā,* | Brightly shining with a halo extending for a fathom, |
| *sabbe te munikuñjarā;* | all these are outstanding sages; |
| *Buddhā sabbaññuno ete,* | all-knowing Buddhas, |
| *sabbe khīṇāsavā jinā.* | all are conquerors, having eradicated the defilements. |
| | |
| *Mahāpabhā mahātejā,* | Of great radiance, great power, |
| *mahāpaññā mahabbalā;* | great wisdom and great strength, |
| *mahākāruṇikā dhīrā,* | greatly compassionate, resolute, |
| *sabbesānaṃ sukhāvahā.* | bringing happiness for all. |
| | |
| *Dīpā nāthā patiṭṭhā ca,* | They are shelters, mainstays, supporters, |
| *tāṇā leṇā ca pāṇinaṃ;* | protections and havens for living beings, |
| *gatī bandhū mahessāsā,* | sanctuaries, kin, great comforters, |
| *saraṇā ca hitesino.* | refuges and well-wishers. |
| | |
| *Sadevakassa lokassa,* | All these are the supports |
| *sabbe ete parāyaṇā;* | for the *devā* and human worlds; |
| *tesāhaṃ sirasā pāde,* | I bow my head at the feet |
| *vandāmi purisuttame.* | of these great beings. |
| | |
| *Vacasā manasā ceva,* | In speech and thought, |
| *vandāmete tathāgate;* | I pay respects to the Tathāgatas, |
| *sayane āsane ṭhāne,* | reclining, seated, standing, |
| *gamane cāpi sabbadā.* | walking, at all times. |
| | |
| *Sadā sukhena rakkhantu,* | May the Buddhas, who show the way to real peace, |
| *Buddhā santikarā tuvaṃ;* | always keep you happy. |
| *tehi tvaṃ rakkhito santo,* | Protected by them, |
| *mutto sabbabhayehi ca.* | may you be freed of all fears. |

| | |
|---|---|
| *Sabbarogā vinīmutto,*<br>*sabbasantāpa-vajjito;*<br>*sabbaveramatikkanto,*<br>*nibbuto ca tuvaṃ bhava.* | May you be freed from all ills,<br>may you be spared all torment;<br>may you overcome all ill will,<br>may you be in final bliss. |
| *Tesaṃ saccena sīlena,*<br>*khanti mettā balena ca;*<br>*tepi tvaṃ anurakkhantu,*<br>*arogena sukhena ca.* | By their truthfulness, virtue,<br>patience, *mettā* and might,<br>may they preserve you<br>healthy and happy. |
| *Puratthimasmiṃ disābhāge,*<br>*santi bhūtā mahiddhikā;*<br>*tepi tvaṃ anurakkhantu,*<br>*arogena sukhena ca.* | In the direction of the east<br>are powerful beings;<br>may they too preserve you<br>healthy and happy. |
| *Dakkhiṇasmiṃ disābhāge,*<br>*santi devā mahiddhikā;*<br>*tepi tvaṃ anurakkhantu,*<br>*arogena sukhena ca.* | In the direction of the south<br>are powerful *devas*;<br>may they too preserve you<br>healthy and happy. |
| *Pacchimasmiṃ disābhāge,*<br>*santi nāgā mahiddhikā;*<br>*tepi tvaṃ anurakkhantu,*<br>*arogena sukhena ca.* | In the direction of the west<br>are powerful *nāgās*;<br>may they too preserve you<br>healthy and happy. |
| *Uttarasmiṃ disābhāge,*<br>*santi yakkhā mahiddhikā;*<br>*tepi tvaṃ anurakkhantu,*<br>*arogena sukhena ca.* | In the direction of the north<br>are powerful *yakkhās*;<br>may they too preserve you<br>healthy and happy. |
| *Puratthimena Dhataraṭṭho,*<br>*dakkhiṇena Virūḷhako;*<br>*pacchimena Virūpakkho,*<br>*Kuvero uttaraṃ disaṃ.* | Dhataraṭṭha to the east,<br>Virūḷhaka to the south,<br>Virūpakkha to the west,<br>Kuvera to the north. |

*Cattāro te mahārājā,*
*lokapālā yasassino;*
*tepi tvaṃ anurakkhantu,*
*arogena sukhena ca.*

These four great kings
are famed guardians of the world.
May they too preserve you
healthy and happy.

*Ākāsaṭṭhā ca bhūmaṭṭhā,*
*devā nāgā mahiddhikā;*
*tepi tvaṃ anurakkhantu,*
*arogena sukhena ca.*

Dwelling in the heavens and on earth
are *s* and *nāgas* of great power.
May they too preserve you
healthy and happy.

*Iddhimanto ca ye devā,*
*vasantā idha sāsane;*
*tepi tvaṃ anurakkhantu,*
*arogena sukhena ca.*

Mighty are the *devas*
living in this teaching.
May they too preserve you
healthy and happy.

*Sabbītiyo vivajjantu,*
*soko rogo vinassatu;*
*mā te bhavatvantarāyo,*
*sukhī dīghāyuko bhava.*

May you be spared all calamities,
may grief and disease perish,
may there be no obstacles in your path;
may you live long in peace.

*Abhivādana-sīlassa,*
*niccaṃ vuḍḍhāpacāyino;*
*cattāro dhammā vaḍḍhanti,*
*āyu vaṇṇo sukhaṃ balaṃ.*

For those of pious nature,
who constantly honor their elders,
four qualities increase:
longevity, beauty, happiness and strength.

## Notes

1 The four assemblies are *Bhikkhus*, *bhikkhunīs*, *upāsakas* and *upāsikās* (monks, nuns, male lay disciples and female lay disciples).

2 The ten strengths of a Tathāgata consist of perfect comprehension of ten fields of knowledge.

3 The four subjects of confidence of a Buddha are that he has attained highest knowledge, that he is freed from all defilements, that he has recognized the obstacles on the path, and that he has rightly taught the way to liberation.

4 The eighteen virtues of a Buddha are: (1) seeing all things past, (2) seeing all things present, (3) seeing all things future, (4) propriety of physical actions, (5) propriety of speech, (6) propriety of thought, (7) firmness of intuition, (8) firmness of memory, (9) firmness of *samādhi*, (10) firmness of energy, (11) firmness of emancipation, (12) firmness of wisdom, (13) freedom from fickleness, (14) freedom from noisiness, (15) freedom from confusion, (16) freedom from hastiness, (17) freedom from heedlessness, and (18) freedom from inconsiderateness.

5 The thirty-two major marks and eighty minor signs are physical characteristics that distinguish a Buddha. The major marks are given at length in *Dīgha Nikāya*, III. 7 (*Lakkhaṇa Sutta*). The minor signs are not listed in the *Tipiṭaka* or its commentaries, although the term for them (anubyañjana) occurs. Apparently the eighty signs were first listed at a later date in works by Myanmar writers.

## Day Two—Ratana Suttaṃ

*In praise of the 'jewels' of the Buddha, the Dhamma and the Sangha, this paritta chanting is from the Sutta Nipāta (2.1), one of the oldest and most popular of the texts in the miscellaneous collection of the Khuddhaka-nikāya. As the introductory verse indicates, it was chanted by the Buddha on the occasion of a famine in the city of Vesāli. This first verse was added later, and the final verse, as presented here, is a contraction of three final verses in the canonical text.*

### Ratana Suttaṃ

*Koṭisatasahassesu, cakkavālesu*
*devatā; yassāṇaṃ paṭigaṇhanti,*
*yañca vesāliyā pure;*
*rogāmanussa-dubbhikkhaṃ,*
*sambhūtaṃ tividhaṃ bhayaṃ;*
*khippamantaradhāpesi,*
*parittaṃ taṃ bhaṇāmahe.*

### Jewel Discourse

[The *paritta*] whose authority is accepted
by the *devas* in the myriad world systems;
which, in the city of Vesali,
the three fears resulting from: disease, non-human beings and famine,
it quickly caused to disappear;
let us recite that *paritta.*

*Yānīdha bhūtāni samāgatāni,*
*bhummāni vā yāni'va antalikkhe;*
*sabbeva bhūtā sumanā bhavantu,*
*athopi sakkacca suṇantu bhāsitaṃ.*

Whatever beings are here assembled,
whether terrestrial or celestial,
may these beings be happy;
moreover, may they carefully listen to these words.

*Tasmā hi bhūtā nisāmetha sabbe,*
*mettaṃ karotha mānusiyā pajāya;*
*divā ca ratto ca haranti ye baliṃ,*
*tasmā hi ne rakkhatha appamattā.*

Therefore let all beings listen!
Have *mettā* for human beings.
Day and night they bring offerings to you,
therefore guard them diligently.

| | |
|---|---|
| *Yaṃ kiñci vittaṃ idha vā huraṃ vā,* | Whatever treasure there is in this world or beyond, |
| *saggesu vā yaṃ ratanaṃ paṇītaṃ;* | whatever precious jewel is in the heavens; |
| *na no samaṃ atthi tathāgatena,* | there is none equal to the Tathāgata. |
| *idampi buddhe ratanaṃ paṇītaṃ;* | In the Buddha is this precious jewel. |
| *etena saccena suvatthi hotu.* | By the utterance of this truth, may there be happiness. |

| | |
|---|---|
| *Khayaṃ virāgaṃ amataṃ paṇītaṃ,* | Cessation of defilements, freedom from passion, and the deathless state, |
| *yadajjhagā sakyamunī samāhito;* | the serene Sage of the Sakyas realized these; |
| *na tena dhammena samatthi kiñci,* | there is nothing equal to this Dhamma. |
| *idampi dhamme ratanaṃ paṇītaṃ;* | In the Dhamma is this precious jewel. |
| *etena saccena suvatthi hotu.* | By the utterance of this truth, may there be happiness. |

| | |
|---|---|
| *Yaṃ buddhaseṭṭho parivaṇṇayī suciṃ,* | That purity praised by the supreme Buddha, |
| *samādhimānantarikaññamāhu;* | called concentration without interruption; |
| *samādhinā tena samo na vijjati,* | there is nothing equal to that concentration. |
| *idampi dhamme ratanaṃ paṇītaṃ;* | In the Dhamma is this precious jewel. |
| *etena saccena suvatthi hotu.* | By the utterance of this truth, may there be happiness. |

| | |
|---|---|
| *Ye puggalā aṭṭha sataṃ pasatthā,* | The eight individuals praised by the virtuous, |
| *cattāri etāni yugāni honti;* | constituting four pairs, |
| *te dakkhiṇeyyā Sugatassa sāvakā,* | these disciples of the Buddha are worthy of offerings; |
| *etesu dinnāni mahapphalāni;* | gifts made to them yield abundant fruit. |
| *idampi saṅghe ratanaṃ paṇītaṃ,* | In the Sangha is this precious jewel. |
| *etena saccena suvatthi hotu.* | By the utterance of this truth, may there be happiness. |

*Ye suppayuttā manasā daḷhena,*
*nikkāmino Gotamasāsanamhi;*
*te pattipattā amataṃ vigayha,*
*laddhā mudhā nibbutiṃ bhuñjamānā;*
*idampi saṅghe ratanaṃ paṇītaṃ,*
*etena saccena suvatthi hotu.*

Those passionless ones, with a steadfast mind,
who apply themselves to the teachings of Gotama,
having attained that which should be attained, plunging into the deathless,
enjoy the peace they have gained without expense.
In the Sangha is this precious jewel.
By the utterance of this truth, may there be happiness.

*Yathindakhīlo paṭhaviṃ sito siyā,*
*catubbhi vātehi asampakampiyo;*
*tathūpamaṃ sappurisaṃ vadāmi,*
*yo ariyasaccāni avecca passati;*
*idampi saṅghe ratanaṃ paṇītaṃ,*
*etena saccena suvatthi hotu.*

Just as a firm post sunk in the earth
cannot be shaken by the winds from the four directions,
so, I declare, is a pure-minded person
who thoroughly realizes the Noble truths.
In the Sangha is this precious jewel.
By the utterance of this truth, may there be happiness.

*Ye ariyasaccāni vibhāvayanti,*
*gambhīrapaññena sudesitāni;*
*kiñcāpi te honti bhusappamattā,*
*na te bhavaṃ aṭṭhamamādiyanti;*
*idampi saṅghe ratanaṃ paṇītaṃ,*
*etena saccena suvatthi hotu.*

Those who have clearly understood the Noble truths,
well-taught by him of deep wisdom,
however heedless they may be,
do not take an eighth rebirth.
In the Sangha is this precious jewel.
By the utterance of this truth, may there be happiness.

*Sahāvassa dassana-sampadāya,*
*tayassu dhammā jahitā bhavanti;*
*sakkāyadiṭṭhi vicikicchitaṃ ca,*
*sīlabbataṃ vā pi yadatthi kiñci.*

With the attainment of the first Path,[1]
three things are abandoned in him:
illusion of self, doubt,
and [clinging to] rites and rituals and such things.

| | |
|---|---|
| *Catūhapāyehi ca vippamutto,*<br>*chaccābhiṭhānāni abhabbo kātuṃ;*<br><br>*idampi saṅghe ratanaṃ paṇītaṃ,*<br>*etena saccena suvatthi hotu.* | He is free from the four woeful realms[2]<br>and is incapable of committing the six heinous crimes.[3]<br>In the Sangha is this precious jewel.<br>By the utterance of this truth, may there be happiness. |
| *Kiñcāpi so kammaṃ karoti pāpakaṃ,*<br>*kāyena vācā uda cetasā vā;*<br>*abhabbo so tassa paṭicchādāya,*<br>*abhabbatā diṭṭhapadassa vuttā;*<br><br>*idampi saṅghe ratanaṃ paṇītaṃ,*<br>*etena saccena suvatthi hotu.* | If he does an unwholesome deed,<br>whether by body, speech, or thought,<br>he is incapable of hiding it, for it is said that<br>such concealment is not possible for one who has seen the state of *nibbāna.*<br>In the Sangha is this precious jewel.<br>By the utterance of this truth, may there be happiness. |
| *Vanappagumbe yathā phussitagge,*<br><br>*gimhānamāse paṭhamasmiṃ gimhe;*<br>*tathūpamaṃ dhammavaraṃ adesayi,*<br>*nibbānagāmiṃ paramaṃ hitāya;*<br>*idampi buddhe ratanaṃ paṇītaṃ,*<br>*etena saccena suvatthi hotu.* | As the woodland grove is crowned with blossoms<br>in the first heat of summer,<br>so the sublime doctrine that he expounded<br>leads to *nibbāna*, highest good of beings.<br>In the Buddha is this precious jewel.<br>By the utterance of this truth, may there be happiness. |
| *Varo varaññū varado varāharo,*<br><br><br>*anuttaro dhammavaraṃ adesayi;*<br>*idampi buddhe ratanaṃ paṇītaṃ,*<br>*etena saccena suvatthi hotu.* | The Sublime One, the knower of the sublime, the bestower of the sublime, the bringer of the sublime,<br>has taught the unsurpassed Dhamma.<br>In the Buddha is this precious jewel.<br>By the utterance of this truth, may there be happiness. |

| | |
|---|---|
| *Khīṇaṃ purāṇaṃ navaṃ natthi sambhavaṃ,* | With the old [kamma] destroyed and no new arising, |
| *virattacittāyatike bhavasmiṃ;* | the mind is unattached to a future birth. |
| *te khīṇabījā avirūḷhichandā,* | The seeds destroyed, the desire [for becoming] does not grow: |
| *nibbanti dhīrā yathāyaṃ padīpo;* | these wise ones go out even as this lamp is extinguished. |
| *idampi saṅghe ratanaṃ paṇītaṃ,* | In the Sangha is this precious jewel. |
| *etena saccena suvatthi hotu.* | By the utterance of this truth, may there be happiness. |

| | |
|---|---|
| *Yānīdha bhūtāni samāgatāni,* | Whatever beings are here assembled, |
| *bhummāni vā yānī'va antalikkhe;* | whether terrestrial or celestial, |
| *tathāgataṃ devamanussapūjitaṃ,* | the Tathāgata is revered by gods and men; |
| *buddhaṃ namassāma suvatthi hotu;* | we pay respects to the Buddha; [by the utterance of this truth] may there be happiness; |
| *dhammaṃ namassāma suvatthi hotu;* | we pay respects to the Dhamma; [by the utterance of this truth] may there be happiness; |
| *saṅghaṃ namassāma suvatthi hotu.* | we pay respects to the Sangha; [by the utterance of this truth] may there be happiness. |

## Notes

1 The first Path is the stage of *sotāpanna*, the "stream winner".

2 The four woeful realms are: i) *Niraya* (the state of woe), ii) the animal realm, iii) the ghost plane, and iv) the demon world.

3 The six heinous crimes: i) matricide, ii) patricide, iii) killing an *arahant*, iv) causing schisms in the Sangha, v) wounding a Buddha, and vi) upholding wrong views.

## Day Three—Karaṇīyametta Suttaṃ

*This paritta chanting, in praise of love and kindness toward all beings, occurs in the Sutta Nipāta (1, 8), and in the Khuddakapāṭha (9). It is entitled Mettasuttaṃ in both occurences. The initial verse was added as part of the paritta tradition and it was called Karaṇīyamettasuttaṃ, a reference to the opening line of the canonical text, in order to distinguish it from other texts also named Mettasuttaṃ.*

| **Karaṇīyametta Suttaṃ** | **Discourse on Practicing Mettā** |
|---|---|
| *Yassānubhāvato yakkhā,* | By the power [of this *sutta*] the Yakkhas |
| *neva dassenti bhīsanaṃ;* | do not show fearful visions. |
| *yañhi cevānuyuñjanto* | A person who is engaged in and practicing |
| *rattindivamatandito.* | [mettā] day and night |
| *Sukhaṃ supati sutto ca,* | sleeps peacefully, and while sleeping, |
| *pāpaṃ kiñci na passati;* | does not have bad dreams. |
| *evamādi guṇūpetaṃ,* | Endowed with these qualities, |
| *parittaṃ taṃ bhaṇāmahe.* | let us recite this *paritta*. |
| | |
| *Karaṇīyamatthakusalena,* | One who is skilled in welfare |
| *yantaṃ santaṃ padaṃ abhisa-mecca;* | and who wishes to attain the ultimate peace, |
| *sakko ujū ca suhujū ca,* | should be able, upright, very upright, |
| *suvaco cassa mudu anatimānī.* | soft-spoken, gentle, and humble. |
| | |
| *Santussako ca subharo ca,* | One should be contented, easily supported, |
| *appakicco ca sallahukavutti;* | with few involvements and few wants, |
| *santindriyo ca nipako ca,* | with senses calmed, discreet, |
| *appagabbho kulesu ananugiddho.* | not impudent, and not be greedily attached to families. |
| | |
| *Na ca khuddaṃ samācare kiñci,* | One should not commit the slightest wrong |
| *yena viññū pare upavadeyyuṃ;* | for which one might be censured by the wise. |
| *sukhino vā khemino hontu,* | May all beings be happy and secure, |
| *sabbe sattā bhavantu sukhitattā.* | may they be happy within themselves. |

*Ye keci pāṇabhūtatthi,*
*tasā vā thāvarā vanavasesā;*
*dīghā vā ye mahantā vā,*
*majjhimā rassakā aṇukathūlā.*

Whatever living beings there may be,
without exception, movable or stationary,
long or large,
medium or small, fine or coarse.

*Diṭṭhā vā ye va adiṭṭhā,*
*ye va dūre vasanti avidūre;*
*bhūtā vā sambhavesī vā,*
*sabbe sattā bhavantu sukhitattā.*

Seen or unseen,
those dwelling far or near,
those who are born and those coming to birth,
may all beings be happy within themselves.

*Na paro paraṃ nikubbetha,*
*nātimaññetha katthaci na kañci;*
*byārosanā paṭighasaññā,*
*nāññamaññassa dukkhamiccheyya.*

Let none deceive another
or despise anyone anywhere;
filled with anger or ill will,
let one not wish any harm for another.

*Mātā yathā niyaṃ puttaṃ,*
*āyusā ekaputtamanurakkhe;*
*evampi sabbabhūtesu*
*mānasaṃ bhāvaye aparimāṇaṃ.*

Just as a mother would protect her only child
with her own life,
even so let one cultivate
boundless love towards all beings.

*Mettañca sabbalokasmiṃ,*
*mānasaṃ bhāvaye aparimāṇaṃ;*
*uddhaṃ adho ca tiriyañca,*
*asambādhaṃ averamasapattaṃ.*

Let one's thoughts of boundless *mettā*
pervade the whole world,
above, below and across,
unhindered, free of hate and of enmity.

*Tiṭṭhaṃ caraṃ nisinno vā,*
*sayāno yāvatassa vigatamiddho;*
*etaṃ satiṃ adhiṭṭheyya,*
*brahmametaṃ vihāramidhamāhu.*

Whether one is standing, walking, sitting
or lying down, as long as one is awake,
one should develop this mindfulness [of boundless *mettā*].
This, they say, is a sublime way of living.

*Diṭṭhiñca anupaggamma,*
*sīlavā dassanena sampanno,*
*kāmesu vineyya gedhaṃ,*
*na hi jātu gabbhaseyyaṃ punaretī ti.*

Not falling into wrong views,
endowed with *sīla* and insight,
discarding sensual desire,
one does not come into a womb again.

## Day Four—Buddha Jayamaṅgala-Aṭṭhagāthā

*This collection of verses is a later composition that has come to be part of the standard inspirational chanting used for the training of young monks and the inspiration of householders. Each of the verses refers to a story, usually drawn from the Pāli commentarial literature, about some event in the life of the Buddha and his disciples.*

| Buddha Jayamaṅgala-Aṭṭhagāthā | Eight Verses of the Buddha's Joyous Victory |
|---|---|
| *Bāhuṃ sahassamabhinimmita sāvudhantaṃ,* | Creating a form with a thousand arms, each bearing a weapon, |
| *Girimekhalaṃ uditaghorasasenamāraṃ;* | Māra [charged], on the trumpeting elephant Girimekhala, surrounded by his fierce troops. |
| *dānādi-dhammavidhinā jitavā munindo,* | By means of virtues such as generosity, the Lord of Sages conquered him. |
| *taṃ tejasā bhavatu te jayamaṅgalāni.* | By the power of such virtues, may victory and happiness be yours. |
| *Mārātirekamabhiyujjhita-sabbarattiṃ,* | More violent than Māra, all night |
| *ghorampanālavakamakkhama-thaddha-yakkhaṃ;* | the fierce, unyielding demon Ālavaka fought. |
| *khantī sudantavidhinā jitavā munindo,* | By means of patience and self-control, the Lord of Sages conquered him. |
| *taṃ tejasā bhavatu te jayamaṅgalāni.* | By the power of such virtues, may victory and happiness be yours. |

| | |
|---|---|
| *Nāḷāgiriṃ gajavaraṃ atimattabhūtaṃ,* | The royal elephant Nāḷāgiri, completely maddened, |
| *dāvaggi-cakkamasanīva sudāruṇantaṃ;* | [sped forth] like a forest fire, a discus or thunderbolt, implacable. |
| *mettambuseka-vidhinā jitavā munindo,* | By means of a shower of *mettā* the Lord of Sages conquered him. |
| *taṃ tejasā bhavatu te jayamaṅgalāni.* | By the power of such virtues, may victory and happiness be yours. |
| | |
| *Ukkhitta khaggamatihattha-sudāruṇantaṃ,* | With upraised sword in hand, implacable, |
| *dhāvanti yojanapath-aṅgulimālavantaṃ;* | Aṅgulimāla pursued him for one *yojana* [about seven miles]. |
| *iddhībhisaṅkhatamano jitavā munindo,* | With a mind prepared by psychic powers, the Lord of Sages conquered him. |
| *taṃ tejasā bhavatu te jayamaṅgalāni.* | By the power of such virtues, may victory and happiness be yours. |
| | |
| *Katvāna kaṭṭhamudaraṃ iva gabbhinīyā,* | Having tied a piece of wood over her belly to feign pregnancy, |
| *Ciñcāya duṭṭhavacanaṃ janakāya-majjhe;* | Ciñca tried to defame him in the midst of an assembly. |
| *santena somavidhinā jitavā munindo,* | By peaceful, gentle means, the Lord of Sages conquered her. |
| *taṃ tejasā bhavatu te jayamaṅgalāni.* | By the power of such virtues, may victory and happiness be yours. |
| | |
| *Saccaṃ vihāya matisaccaka-vādaketuṃ,* | Having strayed from the truth, the wily Saccaka |
| *vādābhiropitamanaṃ ati-andhabhūtaṃ;* | intended to raise the banner of his false doctrine, being completely blinded. |
| *paññāpadīpajalito jitavā munindo,* | By the shining lamp of wisdom, the Lord of Sages conquered him. |
| *taṃ tejasā bhavatu te jayamaṅgalāni.* | By the power of such virtues, may victory and happiness be yours. |

| | |
|---|---|
| *Nandopananda bhujagaṃ vividhaṃ mahiddhiṃ,* | The serpent Nandopananda, [was endowed with] various psychic powers; |
| *puttena thera bhujagena damāpayanto;* | The Buddha's son, the Elder [Mahāmoggallāna], serpent-like, sought to subdue him. |
| *iddhūpadesavidhinā jitavā munindo,* | By means of psychic powers and admonition, the Lord of Sages conquered him. |
| *taṃ tejasā bhavatu te jayamaṅgalāni.* | By the power of such virtues, may victory and happiness be yours. |
| *Duggāhadiṭṭhibhujagena sudaṭṭha-hatthaṃ,* | With arm bitten by the snake of deluded views |
| *Brahmaṃ visuddhijutimiddhi Bakābhidhānaṃ;* | was the Brahma named Baka, pure, radiant and powerful. |
| *nāṇāgadena vidhinā jitavā munindo,* | By means of the medicine of wisdom, the Lord of Sages conquered him. |
| *taṃ tejasā bhavatu te jayamaṅgalāni.* | By the power of such virtues, may victory and happiness be yours. |

## Day Five—Tikapaṭṭhāna

*Day five features chanting of the opening section of the Paṭṭhāna, the seventh book of the Abhidhamma-piṭaka. Paṭṭhāna is a revered text regarded as the highest expression of the Buddha's teaching. Going into far greater detail than the Paṭiccasamuppāda, the Paṭṭhāna examines the twenty-four fundamental relations that govern all phenomena.*

*In the morning chanting of the fifth day Goenkaji chants the Paccayuddeso and the Paccayaniddeso. Because it is a lengthy work, only the Uddeso, otherwise known as the Paṭṭhānamātikā (Paṭṭhāna Matrix) is given here. This list of the twenty-four relations is sometimes recited independently.*

*For a more thorough explanation of the Paṭṭhāna, see Ven. Ledi Sayadaw's Paṭṭhānuddesa Dīpanī (The Manual of Relations), in The Manuals of Dhamma (Vipassana Research Institute, 1999).*

| **Paṭṭhānamātikā** | **Paṭṭhāna Matrix** |
|---|---|
| *hetu-paccayo* | root condition |
| *ārammaṇa-paccayo* | object condition |
| *adhipati-paccayo* | predominance condition |
| *anantara-paccayo* | proximity condition |
| *samanantara-paccayo* | contiguity condition |
| *sahajāta-paccayo* | co-nascence condition |
| *aññamañña-paccayo* | mutuality condition |
| *nissaya-paccayo* | support condition |
| *upanissaya-paccayo* | decisive-support condition |
| *purejāta-paccayo* | pre-nascence condition |
| *pacchājāta-paccayo* | post-nascence condition |
| *āsevana-paccayo* | repetition/frequency condition |
| *kamma-paccayo* | *kamma* condition |
| *vipāka-paccayo* | resultant condition |
| *āhāra-paccayo* | nutrient condition |
| *indriya-paccayo* | faculty condition |
| *jhāna-paccayo* | concentration condition |
| *magga-paccayo* | path condition |
| *sampayutta-paccayo* | association condition |
| *vippayutta-paccayo* | dissociation condition |
| *atthi-paccayo* | presence condition |
| *natthi-paccayo* | absence condition |
| *vigata-paccayo* | disappearance condition |
| *avigata-paccayo'ti* | non-disappearance condition |

## Day Six—Paṭiccasamuppāda

*The following passages, from various sources, offer a dramatic re-creation of events on the night that the Buddha attained liberation. First is the recital of the Paṭiccasamuppāda, the key insight of that night leading to emergence from suffering. Next come the first words of the newly Enlightened One as recorded in the Udāna (I. 13) and the Dhammapada (XI. 89/153154). The concluding verses describe the rejoicing as news of the Enlightenment spread through the thirty-one planes of existence.*

| **Paṭiccasamuppāda** | **Chain of Conditioned Arising** |
| --- | --- |
| ***(Anuloma)*** | **(Forward order)** |
| *Avijjā-paccayā saṅkhārā;* | With the base of ignorance, reaction arises; |
| *saṅkhāra-paccayā viññāṇaṃ;* | with the base of reaction, consciousness arises; |
| *viññāṇa-paccayā nāma-rūpaṃ;* | with the base of consciousness, mind and body arise; |
| *nāma-rūpa-paccayā saḷāyatanaṃ;* | with the base of mind and body, the six senses arise; |
| *saḷāyatana-paccayā phasso;* | with the base of the six senses, contact arises; |
| *phassa-paccayā vedanā;* | with the base of contact, sensation arises; |
| *vedanā-paccayā taṇhā;* | with the base of sensation, craving and aversion arise; |
| *taṇhā-paccayā upādānaṃ;* | with the base of craving and aversion, attachment arises; |
| *upādāna-paccayā bhavo;* | with the base of attachment, the process of becoming arises; |
| *bhava-paccayā jāti;* | with the base of the process of becoming, birth arises; |
| *jāti-paccayā jarā-maraṇaṃ soka-parideva-dukkha-domanassupāyāsā sambhavanti.* | with the base of birth, ageing and death arise, [together with] sorrow, lamentation, physical and mental sufferings and tribulations. |
| *Evametassa kevalassa dukkhakkhandhassa samudayo hotī'ti.* | Thus arises this entire mass of suffering. |

| *(Paṭiloma)* | **(Reverse order)** |
|---|---|
| *Avijjāya tveva asesa-virāga-nirodhā saṅkhāra-nirodho;* | With the complete eradication and cessation of ignorance, reaction ceases; |
| *saṅkhāra-nirodhā viññāṇa-nirodho;* | with the cessation of reaction, consciousness ceases; |
| *viññāṇa-nirodhā nāma-rūpa-nirodho;* | with the cessation of consciousness, mind and body cease; |
| *nāma-rūpa-nirodhā saḷāyatana-nirodho;* | with the cessation of mind and body, the six senses cease; |
| *saḷāyatana-nirodhā phassa-nirodho;* | with the cessation of the six senses, contact ceases; |
| *phassa-nirodhā vedanā-nirodho;* | with the cessation of contact, sensation ceases; |
| *vedanā-nirodhā taṇhā-nirodho;* | with the cessation of sensation, craving and aversion cease; |
| *taṇhā-nirodhā upādāna-nirodho;* | with the cessation of craving and aversion, attachment ceases; |
| *upādāna-nirodhā bhava-nirodho;* | with the cessation of attachment, the process of becoming ceases; |
| *bhava-nirodhā jāti-nirodho;* | with the cessation of the process of becoming, birth ceases; |
| *jāti-nirodhā jarā-maraṇaṃ soka-parideva-dukkha-domanassupāyāsā nirujjhanti.* | with the cessation of birth, ageing and death cease, [together with] sorrow, lamentation, physical and mental sufferings and tribulations. |
| *Evametassa kevalassa dukkhakkhandhassa nirodho hotī'ti.* | Thus this entire mass of suffering ceases. |

| **Udāna-gāthā** | **Verses of Joy** |
|---|---|
| *Yadā have pātubhavanti Dhammā,* | When the [Four Noble] Truths become manifest |
| *ātāpino jhāyato brāhmaṇassa;* | to one of pure life, meditating ardently, |
| *ath'assa kaṅkhā vapayanti sabbā,* | then his doubts all disappear; |
| *yato pajānāti sahetudhammaṃ.* | he understands how each factor arising has its cause. |
| *Athassa kaṅkhā vapayanti sabbā,* | Then all doubts vanish; |

| | |
|---|---|
| *yato khayaṃ paccayānaṃ avedī.* | he has experienced the destruction of the conditions for arising. |
| *Vidhūpayaṃ tiṭṭhati mārasenaṃ,* <br> *Suriyo va obhāsayaṃ antalikkhaṃ'ti.* | Having scattered the army of Māra he stands <br> like the sun, refulgent in the sky. |
| *Aneka-jāti-saṃsāraṃ,* | Through countless births in the cycle of existence |
| *sandhāvissaṃ anibbisaṃ;* | I have run, in vain |
| *gahakārakaṃ gavesanto,* | seeking the builder of this house; |
| *dukkhā jāti punappunaṃ.* | again and again I faced the suffering of new birth. |
| *Gahakāraka! Diṭṭhosi,* | Oh housebuilder! Now you are seen. |
| *puna gehaṃ na kāhasi;* | You shall not build a house again for me. |
| *sabbā te phāsukā bhaggā,* | All your beams are broken, |
| *gahakūṭaṃ visaṅkhitaṃ;* | the ridgepole is shattered. |
| *visaṅkhāragataṃ cittaṃ,* | The mind has become freed from conditioning; |
| *taṇhānaṃ khayamajjhagā.* | the end of craving has been reached. |
| *Jayo hi buddhassa sirīmato ayaṃ,* | The glorious victory of the Buddha has come; |
| *Mārassa ca pāpimato parājayo;* | defeated is Māra the sinful! |
| *ugghosayuṃ bodhimaṇḍe pamoditā,* | From the seat of enlightenment, the victory of the great sage |
| *jayaṃ tadā nāga-gaṇā mahesino;* | was then proclaimed with rejoicing by the host of *nāgas*; |
| *jayaṃ tadā supaṇṇa-gaṇā mahesino;* | by the host of *supaṇṇas [garuḍas]*; |
| *jayaṃ tadā deva-gaṇā mahesino;* | by the host of *devas*; |
| *jayaṃ tadā brahma-gaṇā mahesino.* | by the host of *brahmas*. |

## Day Seven—Bojjhaṅgaparitta

*These verses of protection related to the seven factors of enlightenment are a later compilation from the paritta tradition. They were inspired, no doubt, by the stories of help in sickness received by two of the Buddha's chief disciples, Moggallāna and Kassapa, and by the Buddha himself. These stories are related in the Bojjhaṅga-saṃyutta of the Saṃyutta-nikāya XLVI (V) ii. 4-6, and are referred to in this paritta in the final four verses.*

| **Bojjhaṅgaparitta** | **Protective Discourse on the Factors of Enlightenment** |
|---|---|
| *Saṃsāre saṃsarantānaṃ,* | For beings caught in the cycle of birth and death, |
| *sabbadukkhavināsake;* | for eradicating all their suffering |
| *sattadhamme ca bojjhaṅge,* | and defeating the army of Māra, |
| *Mārasenappamaddane.* | [there are] the seven factors of enlightenment. |
| | |
| *Bujjhitvā ye cime sattā,* | Realizing these seven, |
| *tibhavā muttakuttamā;* | these excellent ones are liberated from the three types of existence |
| *ajātiṃ ajarābyādhiṃ,* | and freed from birth, decay and sickness; |
| *amataṃ nibbhayaṃ gatā.* | they experience deathlessness and fearlessness. |
| | |
| *Evamādi guṇūpetaṃ,* | Endowed with such advantages, |
| *anekaguṇasaṅgahaṃ;* | with innumerable benefits, |
| *osadhañca imaṃ mantaṃ,* | these are words of healing. |
| *bojjhaṅgañca bhaṇāmahe.* | Let us recite the factors of enlightenment. |
| | |
| *Bojjhaṅgo satisaṅkhāto,* | The factors of enlightenment, namely: awareness, |
| *dhammānaṃ vicayo tathā;* | analytical investigation of the Dhamma, |
| *vīriyaṃ pīti passaddhi,* | effort, bliss, tranquillity |
| *bojjhaṅgā ca tathā pare.* | are factors of enlightenment, and the others: |

*Samādhupekkhā bojjhaṅgā,*
*sattete sabbadassinā;*
*muninā sammadakkhātā,*
*bhāvitā bahulīkatā.*

concentration and equanimity.
These seven were well taught,
practiced and cultivated
by the all-seeing Sage.

*Saṃvattanti abhiññāya,*
*nibbānāya ca bodhiyā;*
*etena saccavajjena,*
*sotthi te hotu sabbadā.*

They lead to higher wisdom,
to *nibbāna* and enlightenment.
By this true utterance
may you forever be happy.

*Ekasmiṃ samaye nātho,*
*Moggallānañca Kassapaṃ;*
*gilāne dukkhite disvā,*
*bojjhaṅge satta desayī.*

At one time, the Lord
saw Moggallāna and Kassapa
sick and in pain;
and he preached to them the seven factors of enlightenment.

*Te ca taṃ abhinanditvā,*
*rogā mucciṃsu taṅkhaṇe;*
*etena saccavajjena,*
*sotthi te hotu sabbadā.*

Rejoicing at this,
they were freed from sickness at that very moment.
By this true utterance
may you forever be happy.

*Ekadā dhammarājāpi,*
*gelaññenābhipīḷito;*
*Cundattherena taṃ yeva,*
*bhaṇāpetvāna sādaraṃ.*

Once the King of Dhamma himself
was afflicted by sickness.
He asked Cunda the elder
to recite this very teaching with reverence.

*Sammoditvāna ābādhā,*
*tamhā vuṭṭhāsi ṭhānaso;*
*etena saccavajjena,*
*sotthi te hotu sabbadā.*

And having rejoiced, the Lord
rose up from that sickness.
By this true utterance
may you forever be happy.

*Pahīnā te ca ābādhā,*
*tiṇṇannampi Mahesinaṃ;*

Eliminated forever were the illnesses
of these three great Sages,

| | |
|---|---|
| *maggāhatā kilesāva,* | just as walking on the Path destroys defilements, |
| *pattānuppattidhammataṃ;* | bringing all that is to be attained in accordance with the Law. |
| *etena saccavajjena,*<br>*sotthi te hotu sabbadā.* | By this true utterance<br>may you forever be happy. |

## Day Eight—Mittānisaṃsa

*This poem is taken from the Mūga-Pakkha Jātaka, "The Birth-Story of the Mute Cripple"(Jātaka 538). In this story the Bodhisatta was born as Prince Temiya, son of the king of Kāsī (Benares). In infancy the prince realized that if he ever succeeded to the throne, he would be forced by his position to perform unwholesome actions and therefore to suffer in future. As a way to avoid that, he pretended to be completely paralyzed, deaf and mute. He kept up the ruse so well that after a number of years the king decided that Temiya must be put to death. To be the executioner, the king appointed Sunanda, a charioteer. Sunanda carried the prince off to the forest and started to dig a grave before killing the boy. While he was doing so, Temiya at last decided to drop the pretense and spoke the following poem, asking that his life be spared. Astounded by the prince's revelation of his nature, Sunanda offered to bring him back to court, where Temiya could regain his position as heir to the throne. Temiya refused, however, explaining the reason for his pretense. The charioteer returned alone to the capital to fetch the king and his court. Following Temiya, they all decided to forsake worldly life and become recluses, devoting themselves to purifying their minds.*

| **Mittānisaṃsa** | **The Advantage of Friendship** |
|---|---|
| *Pūrento bodhisambhāre,* | While fulfilling the necessary conditions for enlightenment |
| *nātho Temiya-jātiyaṃ;* | in his birth as Temiya, the Lord |
| *mittānisaṃsaṃ yaṃ āha,* | spoke of the advantage of friendship |
| *Sunandaṃ nāma sārathiṃ;* | to his charioteer named Sunanda. |
| *Sabbalokahitatthāya,* | For the good and benefit of all the world, |
| *parittaṃ taṃ bhaṇāmahe.* | let us recite this protective verse. |
| | |
| *Pahūtabhakkho bhavati,* | Well-feasted |
| *vippavuttho sakā gharā;* | when absent from his home, |
| *bahūnaṃ upajīvanti,* | for many he provides support |
| *yo mittānaṃ na dūbhati.* | he who does not betray friends. |

| | |
|---|---|
| *Yaṃ yaṃ janapadaṃ yāti,*<br>*nigame rājadhāniyo;*<br>*sabbattha pūjito hoti,*<br>*yo mittānaṃ na dūbhati.* | In whatever land he goes,<br>small town or royal city,<br>everywhere he is honored<br>he who does not betray friends. |
| *Nāssa corā pasahanti,*<br>*nātimaññeti khattiyo;*<br>*sabbe amitte tarati,*<br>*yo mittānaṃ na dūbhati.* | Thieves do not overpower him,<br>no prince/king can slight him,<br>he overcomes all enemies<br>he who does not betray friends. |
| *Akuddho sagharaṃ eti,*<br>*sabhāyaṃ paṭinandito;*<br>*ñātīnaṃ uttamo hoti,*<br>*yo mittānaṃ na dūbhati.* | He returns to his home in peace,<br>he is welcomed in assemblies,<br>he is eminent among relatives<br>he who does not betray friends. |
| *Sakkatvā sakkato hoti,*<br>*garu hoti sagāravo;*<br>*vaṇṇakittibhato hoti,*<br>*yo mittānaṃ na dūbhati.* | Being hospitable, he receives hospitality;<br>esteeming others, he is esteemed;<br>he receives praise and fame<br>he who does not betray friends. |
| *Pūjako labhate pūjaṃ,*<br>*vandako paṭivandanaṃ;*<br>*yaso kittiñca pappoti,*<br>*yo mittānaṃ na dūbhati.* | Respecting others, he is respected;<br>honoring others, he is honored;<br>he attains fame and renown<br>he who does not betray friends. |
| *Aggi yathā pajjalati,*<br>*devatāva virocati;*<br>*siriyā ajahito hoti,*<br>*yo mittānaṃ na dūbhati.* | Like fire he shines forth;<br>like a celestial being he is radiant;<br>never abandoned by fortune<br>is he who does not betray friends. |
| *Gāvo tassa pajāyanti,*<br>*khette vuttaṃ virūhati;*<br>*vuttānaṃ phalamasnāti,*<br>*yo mittānaṃ na dūbhati.* | His cattle increase,<br>his fields yield abundant crops,<br>he enjoys the fruit of what he has sown<br>he who does not betray friends. |

| | |
|---|---|
| *Darito pabbatato vā,*<br>*rukkhato patito naro;*<br>*cuto patiṭṭhaṃ labhati,*<br>*yo mittānaṃ na dūbhati.* | Should he fall into a chasm or from a mountain<br>or tree, that man<br>will find firm footing though he is brought low<br>he who does not betray friends. |
| *Virūḷhamūlasantānaṃ,*<br>*nigrodhamiva māluto;*<br>*amittā na pasahanti,*<br>*yo mittānaṃ na dūbhati.* | As a gale [cannot harm] the banyan tree,<br>matured in root and crown,<br>so enemies have no power over<br>one who does not betray friends. |

## Day Nine—Maṅgala Suttaṃ

*Sometimes known as the "vinaya" for householders, the Maṅgala-suttaṃ is very popular in all the Theravāda Buddhist countries. Two traditional opening verses that give some background are often chanted, explaining that devas and men had been discussing for a long time what was a true "maṅgala." The canonical text begins with "Evaṃ me sutaṃ" and tells us the immediate context for the sutta. Goenkaji's chanting on day nine of the course begins with the Buddha's answer (p. 56) to the question put by the devā who came to the Buddha for clarification.*

*The word maṅgala literally means a good omen, a sign of good fortune to come. In this discourse the Buddha explains that the surest sign of future happiness is the performance of wholesome actions now. The sutta is found in Khuddaka-nikāya, Sutta Nipāta, II. 4.*

| Maṅgala Suttaṃ | Discourse on Welfare |
| --- | --- |
| *Yaṃ maṅgalaṃ dvādasahi,*<br>*Cintayiṃsu sadevakā;*<br>*sotthānaṃ nādhigacchanti,*<br>*aṭṭatiṃsañca maṅgalaṃ.* | For twelve years [men] along with *devas*<br>pondered, "What is welfare?"<br>But they did not arrive at<br>the thirty-eight welfares that bring happiness. |
| *Desitaṃ devadevena,*<br>*sabbapāpavināsanaṃ;*<br>*sabbaloka-hitatthāya,*<br>*maṅgalaṃ taṃ bhaṇāmahe.* | The Lord of the *devas* [the Buddha] taught<br>[that which] destroys all evil,<br>for the benefit of the whole world:<br>let us recite those welfares. |
| *Evaṃ me sutaṃ—*<br>*Ekaṃ samayaṃ bhagavā sāvatthiyaṃ viharati jetavane anāthapiṇḍikassa ārāme. Atha kho aññatarā devatā abhikkantāya rattiyā abhikkantavaṇṇā kevala-kappaṃ jetavanaṃ obhāsetvā yena bhagavā tenupasaṅkami. Upasaṅkamitvā bhagavantaṃ abhivādetvā ekamantaṃ aṭṭhāsi. Ekamantaṃ ṭhitā kho sā devatā bhagavantaṃ gāthāya ajjhabhāsi:* | Thus have I heard—<br>At one time the Blessed One was dwelling in Sāvatthi at Jeta's grove, the monastery of Anāthapiṇḍika. Then, indeed, when the night was well advanced, a certain female devā of surpassing beauty, illuminating the whole of Jeta's grove, approached where the Buddha was.<br><br>Having arrived there and respectfully saluting the Blessed One, she stood to one side. Standing to one side the devā addressed the Blessed one in verse: |

*Bahū devā manussā ca,*
*maṅgalāni acintayuṃ;*
*ākaṅkhamānā sotthānaṃ,*
*brūhi maṅgalamuttamaṃ.*

Many *devas* and men
have pondered on welfares,
yearning for happiness.
Please explain what is the highest welfare.

*[Bhagavā etadavoca:]*

[Buddha replies:]

*Asevanā ca bālānaṃ,*
*paṇḍitānañca sevanā;*
*pūjā ca pūjanīyānaṃ,*
*etaṃ maṅgalamuttamaṃ.*

Avoidance of fools,
the company of the wise,
honor where honor is due
this is the highest welfare.

*Patirūpadesavāso ca,*
*pubbe ca katapuññatā;*
*atta-sammāpaṇidhi ca,*
*etaṃ maṅgalamuttamaṃ.*

A suitable place of abode,
the merit of past good deeds,
right aspirations for oneself
this is the highest welfare.

*Bāhusaccañca sippañca,*
*vinayo ca susikkhito;*
*subhāsitā ca yā vācā,*
*etaṃ maṅgalamuttamaṃ.*

Great learning and skill,
well-mastered discipline,
well-spoken words
this is the highest welfare.

*Mātā-pitu-upaṭṭhānaṃ,*
*puttadārassa saṅgaho;*
*anākulā ca kammantā,*
*etaṃ maṅgalamuttamaṃ.*

Serving one's parents,
caring for spouse and children,
a peaceful occupation
this is the highest welfare.

*Dānañca dhammacariyā ca,*
*ñātakānañca saṅgaho;*
*anavajjāni kammāni,*
*etaṃ maṅgalamuttamaṃ.*

Generosity, a life of Dhamma,
caring for relatives,
blameless deeds
this is the highest welfare.

*Āratī viratī pāpā,*
*majjapānā ca saṃyamo;*
*appamādo ca dhammesu,*
*etaṃ maṅgalamuttamaṃ.*

Ceasing and shunning evil,
refraining from intoxicants,
vigilance in the Dhamma
this is the highest welfare.

*Gāravo ca nivāto ca,*
*santuṭṭhi ca kataññutā;*

Respectfulness, humility,
contentment, gratitude,

| | |
|---|---|
| *kālena dhammassavanaṃ,*<br>*etaṃ maṅgalamuttamaṃ.* | listening to the Dhamma at the proper time<br>this is the highest welfare. |
| *Khantī ca sovacassatā,*<br>*samaṇānañca dassanaṃ;*<br>*kālena dhammasākacchā,*<br>*etaṃ maṅgalamuttamaṃ.* | Forbearance, accepting guidance,<br>beholding saintly people,<br>discussion of the Dhamma at the proper time<br>this is the highest welfare. |
| *Tapo ca brahmacariyañca,*<br>*ariyasaccāna-dassanaṃ;*<br>*nibbānasacchikiriyā ca,*<br>*etaṃ maṅgalamuttamaṃ.* | Ardent practice, a life of purity,<br>witnessing the Noble Truths,<br>experiencing *nibbāna*<br>This is the highest welfare. |
| *Phuṭṭhassa lokadhammehi*<br>*cittaṃ yassa na kampati;*<br>*asokaṃ virajaṃ khemaṃ,*<br>*etaṃ maṅgalamuttamaṃ.* | When faced with the vicissitudes of life,[1]<br>one's mind is unshaken,<br>sorrowless, stainless, secure—<br>this is the highest welfare. |
| *Etādisāni katvāna,*<br>*sabbatthamaparājitā;*<br>*sabbatthasotthiṃ gacchanti,*<br>*taṃ tesaṃ maṅgalamuttamaṃ.* | Having acted in this way,<br>everywhere invincible,<br>they go everywhere safely<br>that is the highest welfare. |

## Notes

1 The eight worldly vicissitudes (*lokadhammā*) are: *lābha* (profit) and *alābha* (loss), *yaso* (fame) and *ayaso* (ill repute), *pasaṃsā* (praise) and *nindā* (criticism), *sukha* (pleasure) and *dukkha* (pain).

## DAY TEN—METTĀ-BHĀVANĀ

*The morning chanting of the tenth day features a portion of the practice of mettā-Bhāvanā. The full traditional formula for the giving of mettā is given here. In the morning chanting of the tenth day Goenkaji begins by sending mettā in the ten directions (below). [In the morning mettā instructions of the English only course, he begins the instructions with the first verse below and continues with variations of the following verses.]*

| **Mettā-Bhāvanā** | **Practice of mettā** |
|---|---|
| *[Ahaṃ avero homi,* | [May I be free from animosity, |
| *abyāpajjho homi,* | may I be free from aversion, |
| *anīgho homi,* | may I be free from anger, |
| *sukhī attānaṃ pariharāmi.* | may I preserve myself happy. |
| | |
| *Mātā-pitu-ācariya-ñāti-samūhā,* | Mother, father, teacher, relatives, and everyone— |
| *Averā hontu,* | may they be free from animosity, |
| *abyāpajjhā hontu.* | may they be free from aversion, |
| *anīghā hontu,* | may they be undisturbed, |
| *sukhī attānaṃ pariharantu.* | may they preserve themselves happy. |
| | |
| *Ārakkhadevatā,* | Protective *devas* |
| *bhūmaṭṭhadevatā,* | *devas* of the Earth |
| *rukkhaṭṭhadevatā,* | tree *devas* |
| *ākāsaṭṭhadevatā;]* | *devas* of the sky] |
| | |
| *Puratthimāya disāya,* | In the direction of the east, |
| *puratthimāya anudisāya,* | in the direction of the south-east, |
| *dakkhiṇāya disāya,* | in the direction of the south, |
| *dakkhiṇāya anudisāya,* | in the direction of the south-west, |
| *pacchimāya disāya,* | in the direction of the west, |
| *pacchimāya anudisāya,* | in the direction of the north-west, |
| *uttarāya disāya,* | in the direction of the north, |
| *uttarāya anudisāya,* | in the direction of the north-east, |
| *uparimāya disāya,* | in the direction above, |
| *heṭṭhimāya disāya;* | in the direction below. |

| | |
|---|---|
| *Sabbe sattā, sabbe pāṇā,* | All beings, all living ones, |
| *sabbe bhūtā, sabbe puggalā,* | all creatures, all individuals, |
| *sabbe attabhāvapariyāpannā,* | all having any form of life, |
| *sabbā itthiyo, sabbe purisā,* | all women, all men, |
| *sabbe ariyā, sabbe anariyā,* | all who have attained purity of mind, all who have not yet attained purity of mind, |
| *sabbe manussā, sabbe amanussā,* | all humans, all non-humans, |
| *sabbe devā, sabbe vinipātikā—* | all those in celestial realms, all those in states of woe— |
| *averā hontu,* | may they be free from animosity, |
| *abyāpajjhā hontu,* | may they be free from aversion, |
| *anīghā hontu,* | may they be undisturbed, |
| *sukhī attānaṃ pariharantu.* | may they preserve themselves happy. |

| | |
|---|---|
| *Sabbe sattā sukhī hontu,* | May all beings be happy, |
| *sabbe hontu ca khemino,* | may they all find real security [*nibbāna*], |
| *sabbe bhadrāṇi passantu,* | may all enjoy good fortune, |
| *mā kiñci pāpamāgamā,* | may they encounter no evil, |
| *mā kiñci sokamāgamā,* | may they encounter no grief, |
| *mā kiñci dukkhamāgamā.* | may they encounter no suffering. |

## Group Sittings, Vipassana and Mettā Sessions

*As each day of the course proceeds, Goenkaji chants to open and close the group sittings, and before and after the important teaching sessions of Vipassana and mettā. This chapter presents the daily group sitting chanting day by day.*
*For the group sittings during the first three days of Anapana practice, the opening and closing chanting consists of Hindi dohas. Usually, each dohā is recited twice, with minor variations in the repetition. Only the first version is given here, unless there are significant changes in the repetition. After the fourth day, when Vipassana instructions are given, the chanting changes to a mixture of Hindi and Pāli for the sittings of adhiṭṭhāna.*
*The Hindi invocation that precedes each adiṭṭhāna sitting, "Ananta pūṇyamayi . . .," can be found on pages 66-67. The ending chanting for the adiṭṭhāna sittings is on pages 68-69.*

### Day One

**morning start**

| | |
|---|---|
| *Āo logoṅ jagata ke,* | Come, people of the world! |
| *caleṅ dharama ke pantha;* | Let us walk the path of Dhamma. |
| *Isa patha calate jñāni jana,* | On this path walk the wise ones, |
| *isa patha calate santa.* | walking this path walk the saints. |

**morning end**

| | |
|---|---|
| *Dharama pantha hī śānti patha,* | The path of Dhamma is the path of peace, |
| *dharama pantha sukha pantha;* | the path of Dhamma is the path of happiness. |
| *dharama pantha para jo cale,* | Whoever walks upon the path of Dhamma |
| *maṅgala jage ananta.* | finds infinte well-being. |

**afternoon start**

| | |
|---|---|
| *Āte jāte sāṅsa para,* | In-breath, out-breath |
| *rahe nirantara dhyāna;* | maintain unbroken awareness, |
| *karamoṅ ke bandhana kateṅ,* | the knots of *kamma* will be sundered, |
| *hoya parama kalyāṇa.* | leading to the highest welfare. |

**afternoon end**

| | |
|---|---|
| *Āte jāte sāṅsa para,* | In-breath, out-breath |
| *rahe nirantara dhyāna;* | maintain unbroken awareness, |
| *karamoṅ ke bandhana kateṅ,* | the knots of *kamma* will be sundered, |
| *hoya parama kalyāṇa.* | leading to the highest welfare. |

**evening start**

| | |
|---|---|
| *Dharama dharama to saba kaheṅ,*<br>*dharama na samajhe koya;*<br>*niramala citta kā ācaraṇa,*<br>*śuddha Dharama hai soya.* | Everyone talks about Dhamma<br>but no one understands it.<br>Practicing purity of mind<br>this is pure Dhamma. |

**evening end**

| | |
|---|---|
| *Dharama na hindū bauddha hai,*<br>*dharama na muslima jaina;*<br>*dharama citta kī śuddhatā,*<br>*dharama śānti sukha caina.* | Dhamma is not Hindu or Buddhist,<br>not Muslim or Jain;<br>Dhamma is purity of mind,<br>peace, happiness, serenity. |

## Day Two

**morning start**

| | |
|---|---|
| *Kṣaṇa kṣaṇa kṣaṇa kṣaṇa bītatāṅ,*<br>*jīvana bītyo jāya;*<br>*kṣaṇa kṣaṇa ko upayoga kara,*<br>*bītyo kṣaṇa nahīṅ āya.* | Moment after moment after moment,<br>life keeps slipping by.<br>Make use of every moment;<br>the moment past will never come again. |

**morning end**

| | |
|---|---|
| *Dharama na mithyā mānyatā,*<br>*dharama na mithyācāra;*<br>*dharama na mithyā kalpanā,*<br>*dharama satya kā sāra.* | Dhamma is not blind belief,<br>Dhamma is not wrong action,<br>Dhamma is not false imaginings;<br>Dhamma is the essence of truth. |

**afternoon start**

| | |
|---|---|
| *Sāṅsa dekhate dekhate,*<br>*satya pragaṭatā jāya;*<br>*satya dekhate dekhate,*<br>*parama satya dikha jāya.* | As you observe breath after breath<br>the truth reveals itself.<br>Observing truth after truth,<br>you come to the ultimate truth. |

**afternoon end**

| | |
|---|---|
| *Jo cāhe maṅgala sadhe,*<br>*mukti dukkhoṅ se hoya;*<br>*vaśa meṅ kara le citta ko,*<br>*citta ke vaśa mata hoye.* | If you wish to gain happiness<br>and freedom from suffering,<br>gain mastery over your mind;<br>do not allow it to enslave you. |

**evening start**

| | |
|---|---|
| *Jaba jaba antara jagata meṅ,*<br>*jāge citta vikāra;*<br>*maiṅ bhī vyākula hoṇ uthūṅ,*<br>*vikala karūṇ saṃsāra.* | Whenever in the inner world<br>mental defilements arise,<br>I become agitated<br>and make the outer world agitated. |

*Maiṅ bhī vyākula nā banūṅ,*
*jagata vikala nā hoye;*
*Jīvana jīne kī kalā,*
*satya dharama hai soya.*

May I and may the world
be free from agitation.
This is the art of living,
this is true Dhamma.

**evening end**

*Dekho apne āpa ko,*
*samjho apnā āpa;*
*apne ko jāne binā,*
*mite na bhava-santāpa.*

Observe yourself,
understand yourself.
Unless you know yourself,
the torments of existence cannot end.

## Day Three

**morning start**

*Kāyika karama sudhāra le,*
*vācika karama sudhāra;*
*manasā karama sudhāra le,*
*yahī dharama kā sāra.*

Correct your deeds of body,
correct your deeds of speech,
correct your mental deeds
this is the essence of Dhamma.

**morning end**

*Sampradāya nahīṅ dharama hai,*
*dharama na bane divāra;*
*dharama sikhāye ekatā,*
*dharama sikhāye pyāra.*

Sectarianism is not Dhamma;
Dhamma raises no walls.
Dhamma teaches oneness,
Dhamma teaches love.

*Jāta pāṅtha nahīṅ Dharama hai*
*dharama na baneṅ dīvāra;*
*dharama sikhāye ekatā,*
*manuja manuja meṅ pyāra.*

Caste or rank is not Dhamma,
Dhamma raises no walls.
Dhamma teaches oneness,
love for one and all.

**afternoon start**

*Dekho apane āpako,*
*samajho apanā āpa;*
*Apane ko jāne binā,*
*miṭe na bhava-santāpa.*

Observe yourself,
understand yourself.
Unless you know yourself,
the torments of existence cannot end.

**afternoon end**

*Para sevā hī puṇya hai,*
*para pīḍana hī pāpa;*
*puṇya kiye sukha hī mileṅ*
*pāpa kiye dukha tāpa*

Serving others is virtue,
harming others is sin.
Virtue brings happiness,
sin causes torment.

**evening start**

*Dekho apane āpako,*
*samajho apanā āpa;*
*Apane ko jāne binā,*
*miṭe na bhava-santāpa.*

Observe yourself,
understand yourself.
Unless you know yourself,
the torments of existence cannot end.

**evening end**

*Śīla samādhi jñāna hī,*
*śuddha Dharama kā sāra;*
*Kāyā vāṇī citta ke,*
*sudhare saba vyavahāra.*

*Sīla*, *samādhi* and *paññā*
this is the essence of pure Dhamma,
transforming all actions
of body, speech, and mind.

## Day Four

**morning start**

*Vāṇī to vaśa meṅ bhalī,*
*vaśa meṅ bhalā śarīra;*
*para jo mana vaśa meṅ kare,*
*vahī saccā vīra.*

Good to have mastery of speech,
good to have physical mastery,
but one who is master of his mind
is a true champion.

**morning end**

*Prajñā śīla samādhi hī,*
*maṅgala kā bhaṇḍāra;*
*Saba sukha sādhanahāra hai,*
*saba dukha tāraṇa-hāra.*

Morality, concentration, and wisdom
a treasury of well-being,
conferring all happiness,
removing all misery.

**afternoon start**

*Śīla-dharama pālana bhalo,*
*nirmala bhalī samādhi;*
*Prajñā to jāgṛt bhalī,*
*dūra kare bhava-vyādhi.*

Good to practice morality,
good is right concentration,
good is the awakening of insight
to cure the ills of life.

**afternoon end**

*Śīlavāna ke dhyāna se,*
*prajñā jāgṛta hoya;*
*antaramana kī granthiyāṅ,*
*sabhī vimocita hoṅya.*

When a person of morality concentrates,
insight awakens.
The arising knots of the mind
are all untied.

| Vipassanā-Bhāvanā | Vipassana Instruction Session |
|---|---|
| **Pāli** | |
| *Namo tassa bhagavato arahato, sammā-sambuddhassa. (3x)* | Homage to him, the blessed one, the worthy conqueror, the fully self-enlightened Buddha. |
| **Hindi** | |
| *Jaya jaya jaya gurudevajū,*<br>*jaya jaya kripānidhāna;*<br>*dharama ratana aisā diyā,*<br>*huvā parama kalyāṇa.* | My teacher, may you be victorious;<br>Compassionate one, may you be victorious.<br>You gave me such a jewel of Dhamma<br>which has been so beneficial to me. |
| *Aisā cakhāyā dharamarasa,*<br>*biṣayana rasa na lubhāya;*<br>*dharama sāra aisā dīyā,*<br>*chilake diye chuḍāya.* | You let me taste Dhamma's nectar,<br>now no sensual pleasure can allure.<br>Such an essence of Dhamma you gave,<br>that the shell [of ignorance] dropped away. |
| *Dharama diyā kaisa sabala,*<br>*paga paga kare sahāya;*<br>*bhaya bhairava sāre miṭe,*<br>*nirabhaya diyā banāya.* | You gave such a powerful Dhamma,<br>which helps and supports me at every step.<br>It has helped to rid me of all fears,<br>and made me absolutely fearless. |
| *Roma roma kirataga huvā,*<br>*ṛṇa na cukāyā jāya;*<br>*jīvūṅ jīvana dharama kā,*<br>*dukhiyana bāṭūṅ dharama sukha,*<br>*yahī ucita upāya.* | From every pore such gratitude is pouring<br>I cannot repay the debt.<br>I will live the Dhamma life<br>and distribute its benefit to the suffering people [of the world],<br>this is the only way [to repay the debt]. |
| *Guruvara terā pratinidhi,*<br>*devūṅ dharama kā dāna;*<br>*jo jo āye tapa karaṇa,*<br>*ho sabakā kalyāṇa.* | O my teacher, on your behalf<br>I give the *dāna* of Dhamma.<br>May all who have come to meditate<br>be happy and peaceful. |

| | |
|---|---|
| *Isa dharatī para dharama kī,* | May there be a shower |
| *amṛta varṣā hoya;* | of Dhamma-nectar on this land. |
| *śāpa tāpa saba ke dhuleṅ,* | May it wash away all mental defilements, |
| *mānasa nirmala hoya.* | and purify the minds of all. |

| | |
|---|---|
| *Isa dharatī para dharama kī,* | May there be a shower |
| *amṛta varṣā hoya;* | of Dhamma-nectar on this land. |
| *pāpa tāpa saba ke dhuleṅ,* | May it wash away all mental defilements, |
| *antasa śītala hoya.* | and refresh the minds of all. |
| *Saba kā maṅgala hoya,* | May all be happy, |
| *saba kā maṅgala hoya.* | may all be happy. |

## Pāli

| | |
|---|---|
| *Kammaṭṭhāna* | The Request of Dhamma |
| *Nibbānassa sacchikaraṇatthāya me bhante vipassanā kammaṭṭhānaṃ dehi.* | For the sake of realising *nibbāna*, Sir, grant me the meditation object of Vipassana. |

## Hindi:

| | |
|---|---|
| *Ananta pūṇyamayī,* | Source of infinite merit, |
| *ananta guṇamayī,* | of infinite virtues, |
| *buddha kī nirvāṇa-dhātu,* | [is] the Buddha's element of *nibbāna*, |
| *dharama-dhātu, bodhi-dhātu.* | of Dhamma, of enlightenment! |
| *Śīśa para jāge pratikṣaṇa,* | May it arise on the [top of the] head every moment, |
| *hṛdaya meṅ jāge pratikṣaṇa,* | in the heart every moment, |
| *aṅga-aṅga jāge pratikṣaṇa.* | in every part of the body every moment. |

| | |
|---|---|
| *Ananta pūṇyamayī* | Source of infinite merit, |
| *ananta guṇamayī,* | of infinite virtues, |
| *dharama kī nirvāṇa-dhātu,* | [is] the Dhamma's element of *nibbāna*, |
| *jñāna-dhātu, bodhi-dhātu.* | of wisdom, of enlightenment! |
| *Śīśa para jāge pratikṣaṇa,* | May it arise on the [top of the] head every moment, |
| *hṛdaya meṅ jāge pratikṣaṇa,* | in the heart every moment, |
| *aṅga-aṅga jāge pratikṣaṇa.* | in every part of the body every moment, |

| | |
|---|---|
| *Ananta pūṇyamayī* | Source of infinite merit, |
| *ananta guṇamayī,* | of infinite virtues, |
| *saṅgha kī nirvāṇa-dhātu,* | [is] the Sangha's element of *nibbāna*, |
| *dharama-dhātu, bodhi-dhātu.* | of Dhamma, of enlightenment! |
| *Śīśa para jāge pratikṣaṇa,* | May it arise on the [top of the] head every moment, |
| *hṛdaya meṅ jāge pratikṣaṇa,* | in the heart every moment, |
| *aṅga-aṅga jāge pratikṣaṇa.* | in every part of the body every moment. |

## Closing Chanting, after Vipassanā Instructions

### Hindi

| | |
|---|---|
| *Sādhaka terā ho bhalā,* | O meditator, may success be yours, |
| *ho maṅgala kalyāṇa;* | may you be be peaceful and happy. |
| *aṅga aṅga prajñā jage,* | May insight arise in every part, |
| *jage dharama kā jñāna.* | the wisdom of Dhamma. |
| *Beṭī terā ho bhalā,* | O daughter, may success be yours, |
| *ho terā kalyāṇa;* | may you be be peaceful and happy. |
| *aṅga aṅga jage dharama,* | May Dhamma arise in every part, |
| *anityatā kā jñāna.* | the wisdom of impermanence. |

### Pāli

| | |
|---|---|
| *Bhavatu sabba maṅgalaṃ. (3x)* | May all beings be happy. |

## Adhiṭṭhāna Group Sitting Chanting

*From this point on during the course, the group sittings begin with a Hindi dohā and end with the selection of Pāli verses presented here. Since the end chanting is the same (with one variation for day eight, noted below), only the Hindi starting dohas are given from day five until day ten.*

### Hindi

**evening start**

| | |
|---|---|
| *Śīla samādhi jñāna kī,* | Morality, concentration, and wisdom |
| *bahe triveṇī dhāra;* | three streams have joined and flow together. |
| *ḍubakī māre so tire,* | By plunging into their confluence |
| *ho dukkha sāgara pāra.* | you cross the ocean of suffering. |

| | |
|---|---|
| *Ananta pūṇyamayī,* | Source of infinite merit, |
| *ananta guṇamayī,* | of infinite virtues, |
| *buddha kī nirvāṇa-dhātu,* | [is] the Buddha's element of *nibbāna,* |
| *dharama-dhātu, bodhi-dhātu.* | of Dhamma, of enlightenment! |
| *Śīśa para jāge pratikṣaṇa,* | May it arise on the [top of the] head every moment, |
| *hṛdaya meṅ jāge pratikṣaṇa,* | in the heart every moment, |
| *aṅga-aṅga jāge pratikṣaṇa.* | in every part of the body every moment. |

| | |
|---|---|
| *Ananta pūṇyamayī* | Source of infinite merit, |
| *ananta guṇamayī,* | of infinite virtues, |
| *dharama kī nirvāṇa-dhātu,* | [is] the Dhamma's element of *nibbāna,* |
| *jñāna-dhātu, bodhi-dhātu.* | of wisdom, of enlightenment! |
| *Śīśa para jāge pratikṣaṇa,* | May it arise on the [top of the] head every moment, |
| *hṛdaya meṅ jāge pratikṣaṇa,* | in the heart every moment, |
| *aṅga-aṅga jāge pratikṣaṇa.* | in every part of the body every moment, |

| | |
|---|---|
| *Ananta pūṇyamayī* | Source of infinite merit, |
| *ananta guṇamayī,* | of infinite virtues, |
| *saṅgha kī nirvāṇa-dhātu,* | [is] the Sangha's element of *nibbāna,* |
| *dharama-dhātu, bodhi-dhātu.* | of Dhamma, of enlightenment! |
| *Śīśa para jāge pratikṣaṇa,* | May it arise on the [top of the] head every moment, |
| *hṛdaya meṅ jāge pratikṣaṇa,* | in the heart every moment, |
| *aṅga-aṅga jāge pratikṣaṇa.* | in every part of the body every moment. |

## Pāli

**evening end**

| | |
|---|---|
| *Aniccā vata saṅkhārā,* | Impermanent truly are *saṅkhāras,* |
| *uppādavaya-dhammino;* | by nature constantly arising and vanishing. |
| *uppajjitvā nirujjhanti,* | When they arise and are eradicated, |
| *tesaṃ vūpasamo sukho.* | their cessation brings true happiness. |

| | |
|---|---|
| *Aneka-jāti-saṃsāraṃ,* | Through countless births in the cycle of existence |
| *sandhāvissaṃ anibbisaṃ;* | I have run, in vain |
| *gahakārakaṃ gavesanto,* | seeking the builder of this house; |
| *dukkhā-jāti-punappunaṃ.* | and again and again I faced the suffering of new birth. |

*Gahakāraka! Diṭṭhosi,*
*puna gehaṃ na kāhasi;*
*sabbā te phāsukā bhaggā,*
*gahakūṭaṃ visaṅkhitaṃ;*
*visaṅkhāra-gataṃ cittaṃ,*
*taṇhānaṃ khayamajjhagā.*

Oh housebuilder! Now you are seen.
You shall not build a house again for me.
All your beams are broken,
the ridgepole is shattered.
The mind has become freed from conditioning;
the end of craving has been reached.

*Sabbe saṅkhārā aniccā'ti,*
*yadā paññāya passati;*
*atha nibbindati dukkhe,*
*esa maggo visuddhiyā.*

'Impermanent are all compounded things.'
When one perceives this with insight,
then one turns away from suffering—
this is the path of purification.

**day eight only**

*[Yato yato sammasati,*
*khandhānaṃ udayabbayaṃ;*
*labhatī pīti-pāmojjaṃ,*
*amataṃ taṃ vijānataṃ.]*

[Whenever and wherever one understands
the arising and passing away of the aggregates,
one experiences bliss and tranquility, [which lead on to]
the deathless stage experienced by the wise.]

***Puññānumodanaṃ***

**Sharing merits**

*Sabbesu cakkavāḷesu,*
*yakkhā devā ca brahmuno;*
*yaṃ amhehi kataṃ puññaṃ,*
*sabba-sampatti sādhakaṃ.*

In all the world systems,
may the yakkhas, *devas* and brahmās
rejoice in this merit done by us,
which is productive of all prosperity.

*Sabbe taṃ anumoditvā,*
*samaggā sāsane ratā;*
*pamādarahitā hontu,*
*ārakkhāsu visesato.*

May they all,
unitedly devoted to the teaching,
be without negligence
especially in giving protection.

*Puñña-bhāgamidaṃ c'aññaṃ,*
*samaṃ dadāma kāritaṃ;*
*anumodantu taṃ sabbe,*
*medinī ṭhātu sakkhike.*

The merit gained now and previously
we share equally [with them].
May they all accept with joy,
and may the earth stand witness.

## Day Five

**morning start**

*Gaṅgā Jamunā Sarasvatī,*
*śīla samādhi jñāna;*
*tīnoṅ kā saṅgama hove,*
*pragaṭe pada niravāṇa.*

The true Ganges, Jamuna, and Sarasvati
are morality, concentration, and wisdom.
Where these three streams converge
*nibbāna* manifests.

**afternoon start**

*Mana ke karama sudhāra le,*
*mana hī pramukha pradhāna;*
*kāyika vācika karama to,*
*mana kī hī santāna.*

Correct your mental actions;
mind is first and foremost.
Deeds of body and speech
are offspring of the mind.

**evening start**

*Jaisī cita kī cetanā,*
*vaisā hī phala hoya;*
*duramana kā phala dukhada hī,*
*sukhada sumana kā hoya.*

As is the volition of the mind,
such will be the fruit:
an impure mind yields fruits of misery,
a pure mind gives happiness.

## Day Six

**morning start**

*Śīla dharama ki niṅva hai,*
*dhyāna dharama kī bhīṅta;*
*prajñā chata hai Dharama kī,*
*maṅgala bhavana punīta.*

*Sīla* is the foundation of Dhamma,
*samādhi* forms the walls,
*paññā* is the roof:
the auspicious dwelling of happiness.

**afternoon start**

*Bhogata bhogata bhogate,*
*baṅdhana baṅdhatā jayeṅ;*
*dekhata dekhata dekhate,*
*baṅdhana khulate jāyeṅ.*

Rolling and rolling in sense pleasures
we keep tying knots.
Observing, observing, observing
we open all the knots.

**evening start**

*Main, main, main hī janama kā,*
*jarā mṛtyū kā mūla;*
*ahaṃ bhāva miṭe binā,*
*miṭe na bhava bhaya śula.*

Self-centeredness—this is the root
of birth, decay, and death.
Unless egoism is removed,
the torment and fear of existence will not end.

## Day Seven

**morning start**

*Jyoṅ jyoṅ antara jagata meṅ,*
*samatā stitha ho jāye;*
*kāya vāṇī citta ke,*
*karama sudharate jāyeṅ.*

Whenever in the inner world
equanimity is established,
the actions of body, speech,
and mind are transformed.

**afternoon start**

*Bhogata bhogata bhogate,*
*gāṅṭheṅ bandhatī jāṅya;*
*dekhata dekhata dekhate,*
*gāṅṭheṅ khulatī jāṅya.*

Rolling and rolling in sense pleasures
we keep tying knots.
Observing, observing, observing
we open all the knots.

**evening start**

| | |
|---|---|
| *Jaba taka mana meṅ rāga hai,* | As long as there is craving in the mind, |
| *jaba taka mana meṅ dveṣa;* | as long as in the mind is aversion, |
| *Taba taka dukha hī dukha hai,* | there will be suffering, only suffering; |
| *miṭeṅ na mana ke kleśa.* | the mind cannot be purged of affliction. |

## Day Eight

**morning start**

| | |
|---|---|
| *Dharama hamārā īśavara,* | Dhamma is our master, |
| *dharama hamārā nātha;* | Dhamma is our lord. |
| *hama to nirabhaya hī raheṅ,* | We are always fearless |
| *dharama hamāre sātha.* | if Dhamma is always with us. |

**afternoon start**

| | |
|---|---|
| *Dharama hī mhāro īśa hai,* | Dhamma is my master |
| *dharama hī mhāro nātha;* | Dhamma is my lord. |
| *mhe to nirabhaya hī ravāṅ,* | We are always fearless |
| *dharama hai mhāre sātha.* | if Dhamma is with us |

| | |
|---|---|
| *Dharama hamārā īśavara,* | Dhamma is our master, |
| *dharama hamārā nātha;* | Dhamma is our lord. |
| *sadā surakhśita hī reheṅ,* | We are always well protected |
| *dharama sadā ho sātha.* | if Dhamma is with us. |

**evening start**

| | |
|---|---|
| *Jitanā gaharā rāga hai,* | Deeper the craving, |
| *utanā gaharā dveṣa;* | deeper is the aversion. |
| *jitanā gaharā dveṣa hai,* | Deeper the aversion, |
| *utanā gaharā kleśa.* | deeper is the affliction. |

## Day Nine

**morning start**

| | |
|---|---|
| *Dharama hamārā bandhu hai,* | Dhamma is our kin, |
| *sakhā sahāyaka mīta;* | companion, helpmate, friend. |
| *caleṅ dharama ke pantha hī,* | Let us tread the path of Dhamma, |
| *rahe dharama se prīta.* | giving our love to Dhamma. |

**afternoon start**

| | |
|---|---|
| *Sukha āye nāce nahīṅ,* | Not dancing when pleasure comes, |
| *dukha āye nahīṅ roya;* | not wailing when in pain, |
| *donoṅ meṅ samarasa rahe,* | keeping equilibrium with both |
| *to hi maṅgala soya.* | this is the greatest welfare. |

**evening start**

| | |
|---|---|
| *Mānava kā jīvana milā,* | Achieved this human life; |
| *milā Dharama anamola;* | achieved the priceless Dhamma. |
| *aba śraddhā se yatana se,* | Now with faith and effort |
| *apane bhaṅdhana khola.* | untie the knots of the mind! |

## Day Ten

## Metta Day Chanting

**morning start**

| | |
|---|---|
| *Isa dukhiyāre jagata meṅ,* | In this wretched world |
| *dukhiyā raheṅ na koya;* | may no one be unhappy. |
| *śuddha dharama jaga meṅ jage* | May Dhamma arise in the world, |
| *jana-jana sukhiyā hoya.* | bringing happiness to all. |

***Mettā* introduction**

| | |
|---|---|
| *Dveṣa aura durabhāva kā,* | Of hatred and ill will |
| *rahe na nāma niśāna;* | may not a trace remain. |
| *sneha aura sadbhāva se,* | May love and goodwill |
| *bhara leṅ tana, mana, prāṇa.(2x)* | fill body, mind and life. |

**Hindi *mettā* practice**

| | |
|---|---|
| *Bhalā ho, bhalā ho,* | May all beings be happy, |
| *sabakā bhalā ho.* | be happy, be happy. |
| *Maṅgala ho, maṅgala ho,* | May all beings be peaceful, |
| *sabakā maṅgala ho.* | be peaceful, be happy. |
| *Kalyāṇa ho, kalyāṇa ho,* | May all beings be liberated, |
| *sabakā kalyāṇa ho.* | be liberated, be liberated. |

| | |
|---|---|
| *Sāre prāṇī nirabhaya hoṅ,* | May all beings be free from fear, |
| *nirabaira hoṅ, nirāmaya hoṅ;* | free from animosity, free from disease. |
| *sāre prāṇī sukhī hoṅ,* | May all beings be happy, be happy, |
| *sukhī hoṅ, sukhī hoṅ.* | be happy, be happy. |

| | |
|---|---|
| *Jaise mere dukha kaṭe,* | As my suffering has ended |
| *sabake dukha kaṭa jāṅya;* | may everyone's suffering end. |
| *jaise mere dina phire,* | As my life has improved, |
| *sabake dina phira jāṅya; (2x)* | may the lives of all improve; |
| *jana jana sukha chā jāya.* | may all beings be joyful. |

| | |
|---|---|
| *Bhavatu sabba maṅgalaṃ. (3x)* | May all beings be happy. |
| *Bhalā ho, bhalā ho, bhalā ho* | Be happy, be happy, be happy. |

***Mettā* closing**

| | |
|---|---|
| *Sabakā maṅgala, . . .*<br>*Terā maṅgala, . . .* | May all be happy, . . .<br>May you be happy, . . . |
| *Dṛśya aura adṛśya sabhī,*<br>*jīvoṅ kā maṅgala hoya re. (2x)*<br>*Jala ke, thala ke,*<br>*aura gagana ke; (2x)*<br>*prāṇī sukhiyā hoṅya re. (2x)* | Whether visible or invisible,<br>may all beings be happy.<br>In the water, on land and of the sky, (2x)<br><br>may all beings be happy. |
| *Dasoṅ diśāoṅ ke saba prāṇī; (2x)*<br>*maṅgalalābhī hoṅya re. (2x)* | May all beings in the ten directions, (2x)<br>gain peace and happiness. |
| *Nirabhaya hoṅ, nirabaira baneṅ saba;*<br>*sabhī nirāmaya hoṅya re. (2x)* | May all be free from fear and animosity,<br>May all be free from disease. |
| *Sabakā maṅgala, . . .*<br>*Terā maṅgala, . . .*<br>*Jana jana maṅgala, . . . hoya re.* | May all be happy, . . .<br>May you be happy, . . .<br>May all beings be happy, . . . |

**afternoon start**

| | |
|---|---|
| *Dhanyabhāga sābuna milā,*<br>*niramala pāyā nīra;*<br>*āo dhoyeṅ svayama hī,*<br>*apane maile cīra.* | We are fortunate to have the soap<br>and to have pure water.<br>Come now! We ourselves must wash<br>the dirty linen of the mind. |

**afternoon end**

| | |
|---|---|
| *Maṅgala maṅgala dharama kā,*<br>*phala maṅgala hī hoya;*<br>*antara kī gāṇṭheṅ khuleṅ,*<br>*mānasa niramala hoya.* | The all-auspicious Dhamma<br>bears auspicious fruit:<br>Knots within are opened,<br>the mind becomes stainless. |

**_Mettā_ introduction**

| | |
|---|---|
| *Dūra rahe duraBhāvanā,* | May ill will be far away, |
| *dveṣa raheṇ saba dūra;* | may all aversion be dispelled. |
| *niramala niramala citta meṅ,* | May the pure and stainless mind |
| *pyāra bhare bharapūra. (2x)* | brim over with love. |
| | |
| *Bhalā ho, maṅgala ho, kalyāṇa ho. (2x)* | Be happy, be peaceful, be liberated. |
| *Sabakā bhalā ho,* | May all be happy, |
| *sabakā maṅgala ho. (2x)* | may all be peaceful. |
| | |
| *Sāre prāṇī nirabhaya hoṅ,* | May all beings be free from fear, |
| *nirabaira hoṅ, nirāmaya hoṅ;* | free from animosity, free from disease. |
| *sāre prāṇī sukhī hoṅ,* | May all beings be happy, be happy, |
| *sukhī hoṅ, sukhī hoṅ.* | be happy, be happy |

**_Mettā_ closing**

| | |
|---|---|
| *Mana-mānasa meṅ pyāra hī,* | May rapture spread |
| *urmila urmila hoya;* | through the pool of the mind. |
| *roma-roma se dhvani uṭhe,* | May every pore give forth the sound, |
| *maṅgala maṅgala hoya.* | Be happy, be happy! |
| | |
| *Sabakā maṅgala, . . .* | May all be happy, . . . |
| *Terā maṅgala, . . .* | May you be happy, . . . |

**The afternoon _mettā_ closing, from this point, is the same as the morning _mettā_ closing chanting.**

*Dṛśya aura adṛśya sabhī, . . .* *(see page 73)*

**evening start**

| | |
|---|---|
| *Antara meṅ ḍubakī lagī,* | By plunging deep within, |
| *bhīga gae saba aṅga;* | the entire being has become so saturated |
| *dharama raṅga aisā caḍhā,* | with the color of the Dhamma |
| *caḍhe na dūjā raṅga.* | that no other color can impinge. |

## Day Eleven

***Mettā* introduction**

| | |
|---|---|
| *Mere arjita puṇya meṅ,* | May the merits I have acquired |
| *bhāga sabhī kā hoya;* | be shared by one and all. |
| *isa maṅgala-maya dharama kā,* | May this munificent Dhamma |
| *lābha sabhī ko hoya.* | benefit one and all. |

***Puññānumodanaṃ***

| | |
|---|---|
| *Sabbesu cakkavāḷesu . . . .* | (see page 69) |

| | |
|---|---|
| *Maiṅ karatā sabako kṣamā,* | I pardon all, |
| *kareṅ mujhe saba koya;* | may all pardon me. |
| *mere to saba mitra haiṅ,* | All are my friends; |
| *bairī dikhe na koya.* | I perceive no enemies. |

***Mettā* closing**

| | |
|---|---|
| *Namana kareṅ hama dharama ko,* | Let us pay respects to Dhamma! |
| *dharama kare kalyāṇa;* | Dhamma confers welfare. |
| *dharama sadā rakṣā kare,* | Dhamma always protects us. |
| *dharama baḍā balavāna.* | Great is the power of Dhamma! |

| | |
|---|---|
| *Namana kareṅ saba dharama ko,* | May all pay respects to Dhamma! |
| *dharama kare kalyāṇa;* | Dhamma confers welfare. |
| *dharama sadā maṅgala kare,* | Dhamma always brings happiness. |
| *dharama baḍā balavāna. (2x)* | Great is the power of Dhamma! |

[The two verses above are repeated.]

## Pāli Passages Quoted in the Discourses

### Day Two

*Tumhehi kiccaṃ ātappaṃ,*
*akkhātāro tathāgatā.*
*—Dhammapada, XX. 4 (276).*

You have to do your own work;
Enlightened Ones will only show the way.

*Sabba-pāpassa akaraṇaṃ,*
*kusalassa upasampadā;*
*sa-citta pariyodapanaṃ,*
*etaṃ Buddhāna sāsanaṃ.*
*—Dhammapada, XIV. 5 (183).*

"Abstain from all unwholesome deeds,
perform wholesome ones,
purify your own mind"—
this is the teaching of the Buddhas.

### Day Four

*Niccaṃ kāyagatā-sati*
*—Dhammapada, XXI. 4 (293).*

Awareness always towards the body

*Mano-pubbaṅgamā dhammā,*
*mano-seṭṭhā mano-mayā;*
*manasā ce paduṭṭhena,*
*bhāsati vā karoti vā;*
*tato naṃ dukkhamanveti,*
*cakkaṃ'va vahato padaṃ.*

Mind precedes all phenomena,
mind matters most, everything is mind-made.
If with an impure mind
one performs any action of speech or body,
then suffering will follow that person
as the cartwheel follows the foot of the draught animal.

*Mano-pubbaṅgamā dhammā,*
*mano-seṭṭhā mano-mayā;*
*manasā ce pasannena,*
*bhāsati vā karoti vā;*
*tato naṃ sukhamanveti,*
*chāyā'va anapāyinī.*
*—Dhammapada, I. 1 & 2.*

Mind precedes all phenomena,
mind matters most, everything is mind-made.
If with a pure mind
one performs any action of speech or body,
then happiness will follow that person
as a shadow that never departs.

## Day Five

| | |
|---|---|
| *Jāti'pi dukkhā; jarā'pi dukkhā;* | Birth is suffering; ageing is suffering; |
| *vyādhi'pi dukkhā; maraṇam'pi dukkhaṃ;* | sickness is suffering; death is suffering; |
| *appiyehi sampayogo dukkho;* | association with the unpleasant is suffering; |
| *piyehi vippayogo dukkho;* | dissociation from the pleasant is suffering; |
| *yam'p'icchaṃ na labhati tam'pi dukkhaṃ;* | not to get what one wants is suffering; |
| *saṅkhittena pañc'upādāna-kkhandhā dukkhā.* | in short, attachment to the five aggregates is suffering. |
| *—Dhammacakkappavattana Sutta, Saṃyutta Nikāya, Mahāvagga XII. 2. 1.* | |

| | |
|---|---|
| *Aniccā vata saṅkhārā,* | Impermanent truly are *saṅkhāras*, |
| *uppādavaya-dhammino;* | by nature constantly arising and vanishing. |
| *uppajjitvā nirujjhanti,* | When they arise and are eradicated, |
| *tesaṃ vūpasamo sukho.* | their cessation brings true happiness. |
| *—Mahā-Parinibbāna Sutta, Dīgha Nikāya, II. 3.* | |

## Paṭiccasamuppāda — Chain of Conditioned Arising

*Please see pages 43-44 for the text of Paṭiccasamuppāda*

| | |
|---|---|
| *Aneka-jāti-saṃsāraṃ,* | Through countless births in the cycle of existence |
| *sandhāvissaṃ anibbisaṃ;* | I have run, in vain |
| *gahakārakaṃ gavesanto,* | seeking the builder of this house; |
| *dukkhā jāti punappunaṃ.* | again and again I faced the suffering of new birth. |

| | |
|---|---|
| *Gahakāraka diṭṭhosi,* | Oh housebuilder! Now you are seen. |
| *puna gehaṃ na kāhasi;* | You shall not build a house again for me. |
| *sabbā te phāsukā bhaggā,* | All your beams are broken, |
| *gahakūṭaṃ visaṅkhitaṃ;* | the ridgepole is shattered. |
| *visaṅkhāra-gataṃ cittaṃ,* | The mind has become freed from conditioning; |
| *taṇhānaṃ khayamajjhagā.* | the end of craving has been reached. |
| *—Dhammapada, XI. 8 & 9 (153 & 154).* | |

## Day Six

| | |
|---|---|
| *Sabbe saṅkhārā aniccā'ti,*<br>*yadā paññāya passati;*<br>*atha nibbindati dukkhe,*<br>*esa maggo visuddhiyā.*<br>*—Dhammapada, XX. 5 (277).* | "Impermanent are all compounded things."<br>When one perceives this with insight,<br>then one becomes detached from suffering—<br>this is the path of purification. |
| *Khīṇaṃ purāṇaṃ navaṃ natthi sambhavaṃ,*<br>*viratta-citta-āyatike bhavasmiṃ;*<br>*te khīṇa-bījā avirūḷhi-chandā,*<br>*nibbanti dhīrā yathāyaṃ padīpo.*<br>*—Ratana Sutta, Sutta Nipāta, II. 1.* | With the old [*kamma*] destroyed and no new arising,<br>the mind is unattached to a future birth.<br>The seeds destroyed, the desire[for becoming] does not grow:<br>these wise ones go out even as this lamp is extinguished. |
| *Sabbadānaṃ dhammadānaṃ jināti,*<br>*sabbarasaṃ dhammaraso jināti;*<br>*sabbaratiṃ dhammarati jināti,*<br>*taṇhakkhayo sabbadukkhaṃ jināti.*<br>*—Dhammapada, XXIV. 21 (354).* | The gift of Dhamma excells all gifts,<br>the flavor of Dhamma excells all flavors,<br>delight in Dhamma surpasses all delights,<br>destruction of craving overcomes all suffering. |

## Day Seven

| | |
|---|---|
| *Ye ca Buddhā atītā ca,*<br>*ye ca Buddhā anāgatā;*<br>*paccuppannā ca ye Buddhā,*<br>*ahaṃ vandāmi sabbadā.* | To the Buddhas of the past,<br>to the Buddhas yet to come,<br>to the Buddhas of the present<br>always I pay respects. |
| *Imāya dhammānudhamma-paṭipattiyā,*<br>*buddhaṃ pūjemi,*<br>*dhammaṃ pūjemi,*<br>*saṅghaṃ pūjemi.* | By walking on the path of Dhamma<br>from the first step to the final goal,<br>I pay respects to the Buddha;<br>I pay respects to the Dhamma;<br>I pay respects to the Sangha. |

| Buddha Vandanā | Homage to the Buddha |
|---|---|
| *Iti'pi so bhagavā,* | Such truly is he: free from impurities, |
| *arahaṃ,* | having destroyed all mental defilements, |
| *sammā-sambuddho,* | fully enlightened by his own efforts, |
| *vijjācaraṇa-sampanno,* | perfect in theory and in practice, |
| *sugato,* | having reached the final goal, |
| *lokavidū,* | knower of the entire universe, |
| *anuttaro purisa-damma-sārathī,* | incomparable trainer of men, |
| *satthā deva-manussānaṃ,* | teacher of gods and humans, |
| *Buddho Bhagavā'ti.* | the Buddha, the Exalted One. |

| Dhamma Vandanā | Homage to the Dhamma |
|---|---|
| *Svākkhāto Bhagavatā Dhammo,* | Clearly expounded is the teaching of the Exalted One, |
| *sandiṭṭhiko,* | to be seen for oneself, |
| *akāliko,* | giving results here and now, |
| *ehi-passiko,* | inviting one to come and see, |
| *opaneyyiko,* | leading straight to the goal, |
| *paccataṃ veditabbo viññūhī'ti.* | capable of being realized for oneself by any intelligent person. |

| Saṅgha Vandanā | Homage to the Sangha |
|---|---|
| *Suppaṭipanno Bhagavato sāvaka-saṅgho;* | Those who have practiced well form the order of disciples of the Exalted One. |
| *ujuppaṭipanno Bhagavato sāvaka-saṅgho;* | Those who have practiced uprightly form the order of disciples of the Exalted One. |
| *ñāyappaṭipanno Bhagavato sāvaka-saṅgho;* | Those who have practiced wisely form the order of disciples of the Exalted One. |
| *sāmīcippaṭipanno Bhagavato sāvaka-saṅgho;* | Those who have practised properly form the order of disciples of the Exalted One. |
| *yadidaṃ cattāri purisa-yugāni,* | That is, the four pairs of men, |
| *aṭṭha-purisa-puggalā,* | the eight kinds of individuals, |

| | |
|---|---|
| *esa Bhagavato sāvaka-saṅgho;* | these form the order of disciples of the Exalted One; |
| *āhuneyyo, pāhuneyyo,* | worthy of offerings, of hospitality, |
| *dakkhiṇeyyo, añjali-karaṇīyo,* | of gifts, of reverent salutation, |
| *anuttaraṃ puññakkhettaṃ lokassā'ti.* | an incomparable field of merit for the world. |
| —*Mahā-Parinibbāna Sutta, Dīgha Nikāya, II. 3.* | |

## Day Eight

| | |
|---|---|
| *Phuṭṭhassa loka-dhammehi,* | When faced with the vicissitudes of life, |
| *cittaṃ yassa na kampati;* | one's mind is unshaken, |
| *asokaṃ virajaṃ khemaṃ,* | sorrowless, stainless, secure— |
| *etaṃ maṅgalamuttamaṃ* | this is the highest welfare. |
| —*Maṅgala Sutta, Sutta Nipāta, II. 4.* | |

| | |
|---|---|
| *Katvāna kaṭṭhamudaraṃ iva gabbhinīyā,* | Having tied a piece of wood over her belly to feign pregnancy, |
| *Ciñcāya duṭṭhavacanaṃ janakāya majjhe;* | Ciñca tried to defame him in the midst of an assembly. |
| *santena somavidhinā jitavā munindo,* | By peaceful, gentle means the Lord of Sages conquered her. |
| *taṃ tejasā bhavatu te jayamaṅgalāni.* | By the power of such virtues may victory and happiness be yours. |
| —*Buddha Jayamaṅgala Aṭṭhagāthā.* | |

## Day Nine

| | |
|---|---|
| *Pakārena jānātī'ti paññā.* | Wisdom is knowing things in different ways. |
| —*Paṭisambhidāmagga Aṭṭhakathā* I.1.1 *Ñāṇakathā.* | |

## Day Ten

| | |
|---|---|
| *Atta-dīpā viharatha,* | Make an island of yourself, |
| *atta-saraṇā, anañña-saraṇā;* | make yourself your refuge; there is no other refuge. |
| *dhamma-dīpā viharatha,* | Make Dhamma your island, |
| *dhamma-saraṇā, anaññasaraṇā.* | make Dhamma your refuge; there is no other refuge. |
| —*Mahā-parinibbāna Sutta, Dīgha Nikāya,* II. 3. | |

# Appendix

## Word Meanings of the Pāli Chanting

*The word meanings in the following list are provided to give the reader a simple introductory guide to the vocabulary in the Pāli chanting. This is not a comprehensive grammar. Please refer to a textbook of Pāli for help with case endings, grammar and compound word formation.*

### Namo Tassa *[page 1 and repeated page 7]*

| | |
|---|---|
| Namo ------------------------------------------- | Homage |
| tassa | to him |
| bhagavato | (to the) Blessed One |
| arahato | (to the) worthy conqueror |
| sammāsambuddhassa | (to the) fully self-enlightened One |

### Tisaraṇaṃ Gamanaṃ *[page 3 and repeated page 7]*

| | |
|---|---|
| Ti+saraṇa+gamanaṃ ------------------------- | triple+refuge+going (gamanaṃ=going) |
| Buddhaṃ | accusative. of Buddha |
| saraṇaṃ | refuge/protection |
| gacchāmi | I go to |
| Dhammaṃ | acc. of Dhamma |
| Saṅghaṃ | acc. of Saṅgha |

### Pañcasīla — Five moral precepts *[page 3 - 4]*

| | |
|---|---|
| Pañca+sīla ------------------------------------- | (five+moral precepts) |
| pāṇātipātā | (from) killing living beings |
| pāṇa+atipāta | (living beings+destruction of life, killing) |
| veramaṇī | abstinence |
| sikkhāpadaṃ | rule of (moral) training, precept |
| samādiyāmi | (I) undertake |
| adinnādānā=adinna+ādāna | (from) taking what is not given<br>(that which is not given+taking/seizing) |
| kāmesu | (in) sexual lust |
| micchācārā=micchā+cāra | (from) misconduct (wrong+behavior) |
| Musā-vādā=(Musā+vāda) | (from) wrong/false speech (false+speech) |
| Surā spirituous liquor | |
| Meraya | fermented liquor |

| | |
|---|---|
| Majja | intoxicant |
| pamādaṭṭhānā | (from) causes of heedlessness/intemperate behavior |

## Aṭṭhaṅgasīla — Eight-fold moral precepts *[page 3]*

*The Aṭṭhaṅgasīla follows the order of the Pañcasīla with the following variations and additions:*

| | |
|---|---|
| Aṭṭha+aṅga+sīla | (eight+constituents (of)+moral conduct) |
| abrahmacariyā | (from) incelibacy |
| vikālabhojanā=vikāla+bhojana | (from) eating at the wrong time (wrong/improper time+meal) |
| nacca | dancing |
| gīta | singing |
| vādita | instrumental music |
| visūkadassanā | visiting shows/exhibitions |
| mālā | garland |
| gandha | scent, perfume |
| vilepana | cosmetics |
| dhāraṇa | wearing |
| maṇḍana | adornment, finery |
| vibhūsanaṭṭhānā | (from things for) decoration/embellishment |
| uccāsayana | high bed/couch |
| mahāsayanā | (from using) great /luxurious bed |

## Pariccajāmi — Surrender *[page 4]*

| | |
|---|---|
| Imāhaṃ | this+I |
| bhante | Venerable Sir |
| attabhāvaṃ | individuality, personality, identity |
| jīvitaṃ | life |
| bhagavato | to the Blessed One |
| pariccajāmi | (I) surrender/renounce |
| ācariyassa | to the teacher |

## Kammaṭṭhāna — Request of Dhamma *[page 4]*

| | |
|---|---|
| Nibbānassa | (of) nibbāna |
| sacchikaraṇatthāya | (for the purpose of) realization/experience |
| me | (to) me |
| ānāpāna=āna+apāna | inbreath, outbreath (inhaled breath+exhaled breath) |
| kammaṭṭhānaṃ | meditation object |
| dehi | grant |

## Bhavatu sabba maṅgalaṃ *[page 4]*

| | |
|---|---|
| Bhavatu | may (there) be |
| sabba | all |
| maṅgalaṃ | happiness, beatitude |

## Deva-āhvānasuttaṃ *[no. 2.a, page 6]*

| | |
|---|---|
| Deva-āhvānasuttaṃ | address to the devas |
| Samantā | from all sides |
| cakkavāḷesu | in the world systems |
| atrāgacchantu=atra+āgacchantu | here+may come |
| devatā | devas |
| Saddhammaṃ | true/pure Dhamma |
| munirājassa | of the king of sages |
| suṇantu | may listen |
| saggamokkhadaṃ. | Leading to heaven and liberation |
| Dhammassavaṇakālo =Dhamma +savaṇa+kālo | time to listen to the Dhamma (Dhamma +listening+time) |
| ayaṃ | this |
| bhadantā | respected ones |

## Alternate days Deva-āhvānasuttaṃ *[no. 2.b, page 7]*

| | |
|---|---|
| Ye | those |
| santā | peaceful ones |
| santa-cittā | of peaceful mind |
| tisaraṇa-saraṇā | whose refuge is the triple gem |
| ettha | here, in this world |
| lokantare | other world |
| vā | or |
| Bhummābhummā=bhummā +abhummā | dwelling on earth or elsewhere (terrestrial +non-terrestrial) |
| ca | also |
| guṇa-gaṇa-gahaṇā | merits-multitude-acquiring |
| byāvaṭā | busy |
| sabbakālaṃ. | all the time |
| ete | these |
| āyantu | may come |
| Vara-kanakamaye | excellent gold |
| merurāje | on royal Meru (a mythical mountain) |
| vasanto | dwelling |
| santo | peaceful |
| santosahetuṃ=santosa+hetuṃ | contentment+for |
| munivara-vacanaṃ=muni+vara + vacanaṃ | the words of the supreme sage (sage+supreme + words) |
| sotumaggaṃ=sotuṃ+aggaṃ | to listen+the best |
| samaggaṃ. | together, unitedly |

*[For no. 3., page 7: Namo tassa . . ., see page 83]*
*[For no. 4., page 7:Tisaraṇaṃ Gamanaṃ , see page 83.]*
*[no. 5., page 7]*

| | |
|---|---|
| Imāya | (by) this |

| | |
|---|---|
| Dhammānudhamma | from the first step to the final goal (the law in its fullness) |
| = Dhamma+anudhamma | (dhamma+in conformity with the law/ dhamma) |
| paṭipattiyā | (by) practice |
| Buddhaṃ | acc. of Buddha |
| pūjemi | (I) pay respects/revere |
| Dhammaṃ | acc. of Dhamma |
| Saṅghaṃ | acc. of saṅgha |
| *[no. 6., page 7]* | |
| Ye ------------------------------------------- | Those |
| ca | also, too |
| Buddhā | Buddhas (pl.) |
| atītā | past |
| anāgatā | future (not yet come) |
| paccuppannā | present, existing |
| ahaṃ | I |
| vandāmi | pay respects/homage |
| sabbadā | always |
| Dhammā | dhammas (pl.) |
| Saṅghā | saṅghas (pl.) |
| *[no. 7., page 8]* | |
| Natthi ------------------------------------------- | is not |
| me | mine |
| aññaṃ | any other |
| Buddho (Dhammo, Saṅgho) | nominative of Buddha (Dhamma, Saṅgha) |
| varaṃ | supreme, excellent |
| etena | by this |
| saccavajjena=sacca+vajja | by this true utterance (truth+utterance) |
| jayassu | may there be victory |
| jayamaṅgalaṃ.=jaya+maṅgalaṃ | victory and happiness (victory+happiness) |
| bhavatu | may be, be |
| te | yours |
| sabba maṅgalaṃ=sabba+maṅgalaṃ | happiness, welfare of all (all happiness) |

## Tiratana Vandanā *[pages 8 - 9]*

| | |
|---|---|
| Ti+ratana+vandanā (pl.) | three+jewels, gems+paying respects, homage |
| Itipi=iti+pi ------------------------------------- | Thus also (thus+also) |
| so | he |
| bhagavā | exalted one, freed from impurities |
| arahaṃ | worthy one, one who has killed his enemies |
| sammāsambuddho | fully enlightened by his own efforts |
| vijjācaraṇasampanno=vijjā+ācaraṇa + sampanno | perfect in theory and practice. (theory+practice + endowed with) |
| sugato | faring well, having reached the final goal |

| | |
|---|---|
| lokavidū | knower of the entire universe |
| anuttaro | incomparable |
| purisa-damma-sārathī | trainer of men (charioteer) |
| satthā | teacher |
| devamanussānaṃ | of Gods and humans |
| Svākkhāto=su+akkhāto---------------------- | clearly expounded (well+proclaimed/told) |
| sandiṭṭhiko | to be experienced directly |
| akāliko | giving results here and now |
| ehipassiko | inviting one to come and see |
| opaneyyiko | leading straight to the goal |
| paccattaṃ | individually, for oneself |
| veditabbo | to be realized |
| viññūhi | by any wise, intelligent person |
| Suppaṭipanno---------------------------------- | who are having good practice |
| sāvakasaṅgho | order of disciples |
| ujuppaṭipanno | who are having upright practice |
| ñāyappaṭipanno | who are practicing wisely |
| sāmīcippaṭipanno | who are having proper practice |
| yadidaṃ | that is |
| cattāri | four |
| purisayugāni=purisa+yugāni | pairs of persons (men+pairs) |
| aṭṭhapurisapuggalā | eight kinds of individuals |
| esa | this |
| āhuneyyo | worthy of gifts, of adoration |
| pāhuneyyo | worthy of hospitality |
| dakkhiṇeyyo | worthy of offerings |
| añjalikaraṇīyo | worthy of reverence with clasped hands |
| anuttaraṃ | incomparable, unsurpassed |
| puññakkhettaṃ= puñña+khettaṃ | field of merit (merit+field) |
| lokassa | for the world |

*[Pāli suttas pages 23 - 60]*

## Day 1

## Āṭānāṭiya Suttaṃ

| | |
|---|---|
| Āṭānāṭa | name of town |
| Appasannehi----------------------------------- | unhappy, non-believing, not pleased |
| nāthassa | lord (of, towards) |
| sāsane | teaching |
| sādhugood people | |
| sammate | agreed upon by |
| amanussehi | non-humans |
| caṇḍehi | wrathful |
| sadā | always |
| kibbisakāribhi | evil-doers |
| Parisānaṃ-------------------------------------- | assembly |
| catassannaṃ | four |
| ahiṃsāya | non-hurting |

| | |
|---|---|
| ca | and, also, too |
| guttiyā | protection |
| yaṃ | which, that |
| desesi | taught |
| mahāvīro | of Great valor (Buddha) |
| parittaṃ | protective words |
| taṃ | that |
| bhaṇāmahe | let us recite |
| Vipassī------------------------------------------ | earlier Buddha |
| namatthu | homage |
| cakkhumantassa=cakkhu+manta | endowed with the eye of wisdom (eye+endowed with) |
| sirīmato | glorious |
| Sikhi | earlier Buddha |
| sabbabhūtānukampino=sabba+bhūta + anukampino | compassionate to all beings (all+beings + compassionate) |
| Vessabhū ---------------------------------------- | earlier Buddha |
| nhātakassa | one who has washed off all defilements |
| tapassino | ardent meditator |
| Kakusandha | earlier Buddha |
| mārasenāpamaddino=māra+senā + pamaddino | vanquisher of the army of Māra (Māra+army + vanquisher) |
| Koṇāgamana------------------------------------ | earlier Buddha |
| brāhmaṇassa | of pure life, sinless life |
| vusīmato | perfect one |
| Kassapa | earlier Buddha |
| vippamuttassa | completely freed |
| sabbadhi | in every aspect |
| Aṅgīrasa ---------------------------------------- | resplendent one, radiant one |
| sakyaputtassa | son of the Sakyās (clan) |
| Yo | who |
| imaṃ | this |
| sabbadukkhāpanūdanaṃ=sabba + dukkhā+panūdanaṃ | dispells all suffering (all+suffering+dispell) |
| Ye -------------------------------------------- | who |
| cāpi=ca+api | and also |
| nibbutā | extinguished craving for the world, liberated |
| loke | in the world |
| yathābhūtaṃ | reality as it is |
| vipassisuṃ | insight |
| Te | they, these |
| janā | people |
| apisuṇātha | utter no evil |
| mahantā | mighty |
| vītasāradā | not unexperienced, wise |
| Hitaṃ ------------------------------------------ | benefaction |
| devamanussānaṃ | gods and men |
| yaṃ | whom |

| | |
|---|---|
| namassanti | whom people respect |
| Vijjācaraṇasampannaṃ | perfect in knowledge and moral conduct |
| mahantaṃ | mighty |
| Ete ------------------------------------------- | these |
| caññe=ca+aññe | and others |
| sambuddhā | fully enlightened by his own efforts |
| anekasatakoṭiyo = aneka+sata+koṭiyo | many hundreds of crores (one crore=ten million) (many+hundred+crores) |
| sabbe | all |
| Buddhā | enlightened ones |
| samasamā | equal |
| mahiddhikā | possessing great supernatual powers |
| dasabalūpetā ---------------------------------- =dasa+bala+upetā | endowed with ten types of strength (ten+strengths+endowed with) |
| vesārajjehupāgatā | attained the 4 subjects of confidence |
| paṭijānanti | know |
| āsabhaṭṭhānamuttamaṃ = āsabha+ṭhānaṃ+uttamaṃ | a bull's place i.e. distinguished place (bull+place/position+best) |
| Sīhanādaṃ=sihā+nādaṃ -------------------- | lion's roar (lion+roar) |
| nadante | sound |
| parisāsu | in the assemblies |
| visāradā | skilled, confident, wise |
| brahmacakkaṃ | wheel of Dhamma |
| pavattenti | they roll, start |
| loke | in the world |
| appaṭivattiyaṃ | the movement cannot be turned back |
| Upetā ------------------------------------------- | endowed |
| Buddhadhammehi | (with) qualities of a Buddha |
| aṭṭhārasahi | 18 types of (extraordinary qualities) |
| nāyakā | leaders |
| battiṃsa-lakkhaṇūpetā=battiṃsa + lakkhaṇa+upetā | endowed with 32 marks (32+marks + endowed with) |
| sītānubyañjanādharā | having 80 smaller marks |
| Byāmappabhāya=byāma+pabhāya ---------- | fathom+halo (with) |
| suppabhā | brightly glowing |
| muni+kuñjarā | (sage+outstanding elephant) |
| sabbaññuno | all knowing, omniscient |
| khīṇāsavā = khīṇa+āsavā | arahants, who have eradicated all defilements (exhausted+that which flows (mental defilements) |
| jinā | conquerors |
| Mahāpabhā ------------------------------------ | of great radiance |
| mahātejā | of great power |
| mahāpaññā | of great wisdom |
| mahabbalā | of great strength |
| mahākāruṇikā | of great compassion |
| dhīrā | resolute |
| sabbesānaṃ | for all |

| | |
|---|---|
| sukhāvahā | bringing happiness |
| Dīpā ---------- | shelter, island |
| nāthā | protections, Lords |
| patiṭṭhā | help, resting place, shelter |
| tāṇā | protection |
| leṇā | harbor |
| pāṇinaṃ. | for living beings |
| gatī | sanctuaries/refuges |
| bandhū | kin, relatives |
| mahessāsā (mahā+assāsa) | great+comfort |
| saraṇā | refuges |
| hitesino | well wishers |
| Sadevakassa ---------- | with all the devas |
| lokassa | of this world |
| parāyaṇā | support |
| sirasā | with head |
| pāde | at the feet |
| vandāmi | I bow |
| purisuttame | excellent men, great beings |
| Vacasā ---------- | in speech |
| manasā | in thought |
| ceva=ca+eva | and also (and+also) |
| vandāmete=vandāmi+ete | I pay respect to these (I bow down to+these) |
| tathāgate | Buddhas |
| sayane | while reclining |
| āsane | while seated |
| ṭhāne | while standing |
| gamane | while walking |
| sabbadā | all the time |
| Sadā ---------- | always |
| sukhena | happily |
| rakkhantu | preserve, keep |
| santikarā | who shows the way to (promotes) peace |
| tehi | by them |
| tvaṃ | you |
| rakkhito | protected |
| santo | peaceful |
| mutt o | free |
| sabbabhayehi=sabba+bhayehi | from all fears (all+from fears) |
| Sabbarogā ---------- | from all ills |
| vinīmutto | completely free |
| sabbasantāpavajjito=sabba+santāpa + vajjito | spared all torment (all+torment + avoided/spared by) |
| sabbaveramatikkanto | overcome all hatred (all+hatred+overcome) |
| nibbuto | extinguished, quenched, to be in final bliss |
| bhava | be, become |
| Tesaṃ ---------- | their |
| saccena | truth |

| | |
|---|---|
| sīlena | virtue |
| khanti | patience |
| mettā | loving-kindness |
| balena | might |
| tepi=te+pi | they also (they+also) |
| tvaṃ | you |
| anurakkhantu | may they protect, may they preserve |
| arogena | healthy |
| sukhena | happiness |
| Puratthimasmiṃ | in the eastern direction |
| disābhāge | directions |
| santi | there are |
| bhūtā | beings |
| Dakkhiṇasmiṃ | in the southern direction |
| Pacchimasmiṃ | in the western direction |
| nāgā | serpents |
| Uttarasmiṃ | in the northern direction |
| yakkhā | non-human being, demon |
| Dhataraṭṭho | king of the east (name) |
| Virūḷhako | king of the south (name) |
| Virūpakkho | king of the west (name) |
| Kuvero | king of the north (name) |
| Cattāro | four |
| mahārājā | great kings |
| lokapālā=loka+pāla | guardians of this world (world+protectors) |
| yasassino | having fame |
| Ākāsaṭṭhā | dwelling in the sky |
| bhummaṭṭhā | dwelling on earth |
| Iddhimanto | mighty/powerful ones |
| ye | those |
| vasantā | living |
| idha | here |
| sāsane | in the teaching/dispensation |
| Sabbītiyo=sabba+īti | all calamities |
| vivajjantu | (may) go away |
| soko | grief |
| rogo | disease |
| vinassatu | may get destroyed, perish |
| mā | not |
| bhavatvantarāyo=bhavatu+antarāyo | harm befall on (be+harm) |
| sukhī | happy |
| dīghāyuko | long life |
| Abhivādanasīlassa | the habit of respectful salutation |
| niccaṃ | always |

| | |
|---|---|
| vuḍḍhāpacāyino (vuḍḍhā+ apacāyino) | respecting elders (old/aged+those who respect) |
| dhammā | qualities |
| vaḍḍhanti | increase |
| āyu | age, longevity |
| vaṇṇo | beauty, complexion |
| sukhaṃ | happiness |
| balaṃ | strength |

## Day 2

## Ratana Suttaṃ

| | |
|---|---|
| Koṭisatasahassesu=Koṭi+sata +sahassa --------------- | extremely high figure (crore+hundred +thousand) |
| cakkavāḷesu | in the world systems |
| devatā | devas |
| Yassāṇaṃ=yassa+āṇaṃ | whose command (whose+command) |
| paṭigaṇhanti | accept |
| yañca=yaṃ+ca | and which (which+and) |
| vesāliyā | in Vesāli (a city) |
| pure | previously |
| rogāmanussa-dubbhikkhaṃ=roga + amanussa+dubbhikkhaṃ | disease+non-human+famine |
| sambhūtaṃ | arisen from these |
| tividhaṃ | 3 types |
| bhayaṃ | fear |
| Khippamantaradhāpesi (Khippaṃ + antaradhāpesi) | quickly caused to disappear (quickly + caused to disappear) |
| parittaṃ | protective verse |
| taṃ | that |
| bhaṇāmahe | let us recite |
| Yānīdha=yāni+idha--------------------------- | whatever+here |
| bhūtāni | living beings |
| samāgatāni | are gathered |
| bhummāni | earth bound |
| vā | or, whether |
| antalikkhe. | celestial (the sky) |
| sabbeva | all |
| bhūtā | beings |
| sumanā | happy |
| bhavantu | be |
| athopi=atho+api | and (then also) |
| sakkacca | respectfully, carefully |
| suṇantu | may listen |
| bhāsitaṃ. | these words, that which is spoken |
| Tasmā------------------------------------------- | therefore |
| hi | indeed |

| | |
|---|---|
| nisāmetha | listen |
| sabbe | all |
| mettaṃ | mettā |
| karotha | practice |
| mānusiyā | toward human |
| pajāya | beings |
| divā | day |
| ca | and |
| ratto | night |
| haranti | carry |
| ye | who |
| baliṃ | offering |
| ne | them |
| rakkhatha | protect |
| appamattā | diligently |
| Yaṃ ------------------------------------------ | what, that |
| kiñci | something, whatsoever |
| vittaṃ | wealth |
| idha | here |
| huraṃ | beyond |
| saggesu | heavens (in the) |
| ratanaṃ | gem, jewel |
| paṇītaṃ. | excellent, precious |
| na | not |
| no | no |
| samaṃ | equal to |
| atthi | is |
| tathāgatena | the Buddha |
| idampi=idaṃ+pi | this too (this+also) |
| etena | by (the power of) this |
| saccena | (by this) truth |
| suvatthi | well-being |
| hotu | be (may there be) |
| Khayaṃ ---------------------------------------- | cessation |
| virāgaṃ | detachment |
| amataṃ | deathless state |
| yadajjhagā=yaṃ+ajjhagā | (which+attained) |
| sakyamunī=sakya+munī | Sakyan sage (Sakyan+sage) |
| samāhito | well concentrated |
| tena | this, that |
| dhammena | state |
| samatthi=sama+atthi | equal to+is |
| dhamme | in Dhamma |
| buddhaseṭṭho=Buddha+seṭṭho -------------- | Buddha+supreme, foremost |
| parivaṇṇayī | praised by |
| suciṃ | purity |

| | |
|---|---|
| samādhimānantarikaññamāhu = samādhiṃ+ānantarika + aññaṃ+āhu | concentration (that accompanies path consciousness) described by the Buddhas as giving result immediately (concentration+immediately following+other+which is called) |
| samo | equal |
| vijjati | is |
| puggalā | individual |
| aṭṭha | eight |
| sataṃ | by the wise |
| pasatthā | praised |
| cattāri | four |
| etāni | those |
| yugāni | pairs |
| honti | are |
| Te | they |
| dakkhiṇeyyā | worthy of offerings |
| sugatassa | of Buddha |
| sāvakā | disciples |
| etesu | to these |
| dinnāni | whatever is offered |
| mahapphalāni | great fruit |
| saṅghe | in the Saṅgha |
| suppayuttā | who engage themselves |
| manasā | mind (with) |
| daḷhena | firm |
| nikkāmino | those free from craving |
| gotamasāsanamhi | in the teaching of the Buddha |
| pattipattā=patti+pattā | having attained the goal (to be attained+attained) |
| vigayha | experience |
| laddhā | thus obtained |
| mudhā | without expense, gratis |
| nibbutiṃ | peace |
| bhuñjamānā | enjoying |
| Yathindakhīlo=yathā+inda+khīlo | just as+Indra (highest devā)+pillar |
| paṭhaviṃ | in the earth |
| sito | planted (fixed) |
| siyā | may be |
| catubbhi | from four (directions) |
| vātehi | winds (by) |
| asampakampiyo | cannot be shaken |
| tathūpamaṃ=tathā+upamaṃ | likewise+comparison |
| sappurisaṃ | pure minded person |
| vadāmi | I declare |
| yo | who |
| ariyasaccāni | noble truths |
| avecca | fully |
| passati | realizes |
| vibhāvayanti | clearly understand |

| | |
|---|---|
| gambhīrapaññena=gambhīra+paññena | deep wisdom (deep+by the one endowed with wisdom) |
| sudesitāni | well taught |
| kiñcāpi | however much, whatsoever |
| bhusappamattā=bhusa+pamattā | much careless |
| bhavaṃ | birth |
| aṭṭhamamādiyanti=aṭṭhamaṃ+ādiyanti | eighth+take |
| Sahāvassa ------------------------------------ | simultaneously with |
| dassana-sampadāya | insight-attainment |
| tayassu | three |
| dhammā | things, factors, qualities (in this context, the 3 fetters) |
| jahitā | dropped off, abandoned |
| bhavanti | become |
| sakkāyadiṭṭhi | (1) illusion of self |
| vicikicchitaṃ | (2) doubt |
| sīlabbataṃ=sīla+vata | (3) rites and rituals (rules, precepts+vow, rites) |
| pi (fr. api) | also |
| yadatthi | if any |
| Catūhapāyehi=catuhi+apāyehi--------------- | 4 spheres of existence below the human realm (from four+from lower worlds) |
| vippamutto | completely freed |
| chaccābhiṭhānāni=cha+ca + abhiṭhānāni | 6 heinous crimes (6+and +heinous crimes) |
| abhabbo | incapable |
| kātuṃ. | doing, to do |
| so -------------------------------------------- | he |
| kammaṃ | deed |
| karoti | he commits |
| pāpakaṃ | unwholesome |
| kāyena | by body |
| vācā | by speech |
| uda | or |
| cetasā | by thought (mind) |
| paṭicchādāya | concealing |
| abhabbatā | incapability |
| diṭṭhapadassa | of one who has seen the abode (nibbāna) |
| vuttā | it is said |
| Vanappagumbe--------------------------------- | forest bush, grove |
| yathā | as |
| phussitagge | blossoms |
| gimhānamāse=gimhāna+māse | in the summer month (summer+in the month) |
| paṭhamasmiṃ | first (in the) |
| gimhe | hot season |
| dhammavaraṃ=dhammaṃ+ varaṃ | sublime Dhamma (dhamma+sublime) |
| adesayi | expounded |
| nibbānagāmiṃ | leading to nibbāna |

paramaṃ greatest
hitāya for the good
Varo -------------------------------------------the sublime one
varaññū knower of the sublime
varado giver of the sublime
varāharo bringer of the sublime
anuttaro unsurpassed
khīṇaṃ ----------------------------------------destroyed
purāṇaṃ old
navaṃ new, fresh
natth is not
sambhavaṃ is produced
virattacittāyatike=viratta+citta +āyatike mind detached from future (detached from +mind+future)
bhavasmiṃ. birth
khīṇabījā destroyed seed
avirūḷhichandā=avirūḷhi+chandā cessation of growth of cravings (no longer arise +cravings)
nibbanti cease
dhīrā wise ones
yathā'yaṃ=yathā+ayaṃ just as this
padīpo flame, lamp
Tathāgataṃ ------------------------------------the Buddha
devamanussapūjitaṃ=devā+manussa +pūjitaṃ honored by devas and men (devas+men +honored)
namassāma we pay respects
suvatthi well being

## Day 3

## Karaṇīyamettā Suttaṃ

Karaṇīya something that should be done
Yassānubhāvato=Yassa+ānubhāvato --------by whose+power, greatness, majesty
yakkhā unseen beings, most are hostile but some are helpful
neva=na+eva never (not+even)
dassenti show
bhīsanaṃ. dreadful sights (forms)
yañhi that indeed
cevānuyuñjanto=ca+eva + anuyuñjanto and+also+practicing
rattindivamatandito=rattiṃ+divaṃ + atandito night and day, diligently (in the night + in the day+without drowsiness)
sukhaṃ happily
supati sleeps
sutto slept
ca and

| | |
|---|---|
| pāpaṃ | evil |
| kiñci | anything |
| na | not |
| passati. | to see |
| evamādi=evaṃ+ādi | like this+etc. |
| guṇūpetaṃ | endowed with these good qualities |
| parittaṃ | protection |
| taṃ | that |
| bhaṇāmahe | let us chant |
| Karaṇīyam-atthakusalena -------------------- = Karaṇīyaṃ+attha+kusalena | someone who knows that his welfare depends on this, he is proficient. (something to bedone +welfare/advantage+proficient) |
| yantaṃ=yaṃ+taṃ | that which (which+that) |
| santaṃ | peaceful |
| padaṃ | state |
| abhisamecca. | would attain |
| sakko | capable |
| ujū | honest, straightforward |
| suhujū | upright |
| suvaco | soft spoken |
| cassa=ca+assa | should also be (and+may be) |
| mudu | gentle |
| anatimānī | humble |
| Santussako ------------------------------------- | contented |
| subharo | live modestly |
| appakicco | having few duties |
| sallahukavutti. | simple livelihood |
| santindriyo=santa+indriya | controlled in senses (peaceful+faculty/senses) |
| nipako | prudent, wise |
| appagabbho | retiring, not aggressive |
| kulesvananugiddho=kulesu + ananugiddho | not greedy for supporters (toward families + not greedy) |
| khuddaṃ samācare ---------------------------- | small, inferior+to do, perform |
| yena | by which |
| viññū | the wise |
| pare | later |
| upavadeyyuṃ. | censure |
| sukhino | happy |
| vā | or |
| khemino | secure |
| hontu | be |
| sabbe | all |
| sattā | beings |
| bhavantu | be |
| sukhitattā=sukhita+attā | happy+themselves |
| Ye -------------------------------------------- | who |
| keci | whatever |
| pāṇabhūtatthi=pāṇabhūta+atthi | living beings+there are |

| | |
|---|---|
| tasā | movable |
| thāvarā | stationary |
| vanavasesā=vā+anavasesā | excluding none |
| dīghā | long |
| vā | so |
| ye | those, whoever |
| mahantā | great |
| majjhimā | middling |
| rassakā | short |
| aṇukathūlā=aṇuka+thūla | subtle or gross (subtle+gross) |
| Diṭṭhā ------------------------------------------ | seen |
| adiṭṭhā | unseen |
| dūre | far |
| vasanti | dwelling |
| avidūre | near |
| bhūtā | born |
| sambhavesī | seeking birth, due to be born |
| sattā | beings |
| paro ------------------------------------------ | one |
| paraṃ | another |
| nikubbetha | (may) deceive |
| nātimaññetha=na+atimaññetha | not despise (not+may despise) |
| katthaci | anywhere |
| na | not |
| kañci | anyone |
| byārosanā | out of anger |
| paṭighasaññā | ill will (anger+gesture/perception) |
| nāññamaññassa=na+aññamaññassa | (not+of one another) |
| dukkhamiccheyya=dukkhaṃ+ iccheyya | wish for suffering (suffering+wish for) |
| Mātā ------------------------------------------ | mother |
| yathā | just as |
| niyaṃ | own (one's) |
| puttaṃ | child |
| āyusā | with one's life |
| ekaputtamanurakkhe = eka+puttaṃ+anurakkhe | (only+child+would protect) |
| evampi=evaṃ+pi | even so (so+also) |
| sabbabhūtesu=sabba+bhūtesu | towards all beings (all+toward beings) |
| mānasaṃ | mind |
| bhāvaye | cultivate |
| aparimāṇaṃ. | boundless |
| Mettañca=mettaṃ+ca ------------------------ | goodwill, loving-kindness+and |
| sabba lokasmiṃ | in the entire universe |
| uddhaṃ | above |
| adho | below |
| tiriyañca | and across |
| asambādhaṃ | without obstruction |

| | |
|---|---|
| averamasapattaṃ=averaṃ+asapattaṃ | without hatred+without enmity |
| Tiṭṭhaṃ ------------------------------------------- | (while) standing |
| caraṃ | walking |
| nisinno | sitting |
| sayāno | lying |
| yāvatassa | as long as |
| vigatamiddho=vigata+middho | one who is awake (free from+drowsiness) |
| etaṃ | this |
| satiṃ | awareness |
| adhiṭṭheyya | practice, fix one's attention |
| brahmam-etaṃ | sublime/brahmic+this |
| vihāramidhamāhu=vihāraṃ-idhaṃ-āhu | the dwelling+here (in the dispensation of the Buddha)+they have said |
| Diṭṭhiñca=diṭṭhiṃ+ca ------------------------- | (false) view+and |
| anupaggamma=ana+upaggamma | not succumbing (not+falling into) |
| sīlavā | established in moral conduct |
| dassanena | insight |
| sampanno | endowed with |
| kāmesu | sensual |
| vineyya | having removed |
| gedhaṃ | craving |
| hi | yes, indeed |
| jātu | surely, undoubtedly |
| gabbhaseyyaṃ=gabbha+seyyaṃ | womb+lying down |
| punareti | come again |

## Day 4

## Buddha Jayamaṅgala-aṭṭhagāthā

| | |
|---|---|
| Bāhuṃ ------------------------------------------- | arm |
| Sahassamabhinimmita=sahassaṃ + abhinimmita | creating (a form with) one thousand (arms) (thousand+creating) |
| sāvudhantaṃ | bearing weapons |
| girimekhalaṃ | name of an elephant |
| uditaghorasasenamāraṃ.= udita+ghora + sasena+māraṃ | the fierce Māra surrounded by his army (charged/risen+fierce+with army+māra) |
| Dānādi-dhammavidhinā | by means of virtues such as generosity |
| = Dāna+ādi+Dhamma+vidhinā(generosity+such as+qualities+by means of) | |
| jitavā | conqueror |
| munindo | the great sage |
| taṃ | that |
| tejasā | by the power of |
| bhavatu | may be |
| te | yours |

| | |
|---|---|
| jayamaṅgalāni | victory and happiness |
| Mārātirekamabhiyujjhita --------------------- | fought more ardently than Māra |
| =Māra+atirekaṃ+abhiyujjhita -- | (Māra+more than+fought ardently) |
| sabbarattiṃ | all night |
| ghorampanālavakaṃakkhamathaddha | the intolerant, unyielding demon named Ālavaka |
| ghoram+pana+ālavakam | fierce+but+name of a Yakkha |
| + akkhama+thaddha | + intolerant+hard |
| yakkhaṃ | non-human being, demon |
| khantī | patience |
| sudantavidhinā | by means of self-control |
| Nāḷāgiriṃ -------------------------------------- | name of an elephant |
| gajavaraṃ=gaja+varaṃ | royal/noble elephant (elephant+stately) |
| atimattabhūtaṃ=ati+matta+bhūtaṃ | having become too mad (very+intoxicated + having become) |
| dāvaggi-cakkamasanīva=dāva + aggi+cakkaṃ+asani+iva | like a forest fire, discus or a thunderbolt (forest + fire+discus+thunderbolt+like) |
| sudāruṇantaṃ. | implacable |
| mettambusekavidhinā=mettā+ambu + seka+vidhinā | by sprinkling the water of mettā (mettā+water + sprinkling+by means of) |
| Ukkhitta----------------------------------------- | upraised |
| khaggamatihattha=khaggaṃ+atihattha | sword in hand (sword+bringing) |
| dhāvanti | pursued |
| yojanapathaṅgulimālavantaṃ=yojana patha+aṅgulimāla+vantaṃ | Angulimāla pursued him for 3 leagues (ca. 7 miles + range of+Angulimāla + renounced/left behind) |
| iddhībhisaṅkhatamano=iddhībhi + saṅkhata+mano | with a mind expert in marvels (with magical powers+expert+mind) |
| Katvāna ---------------------------------------- | doing |
| kaṭṭhamudaraṃ=kaṭṭhaṃ+udaraṃ | piece of wood+on the belly |
| iva | like |
| gabbhinīyā | pregnant woman |
| ciñcāya | by Ciñcā (name of girl) |
| duṭṭhavacanaṃ=duṭṭha+vacanaṃ | wicked speech (wicked+speech) |
| janakāya | assembly of people |
| majjhe | in the midst of |
| santena | by peaceful |
| somavidhinā=somma+vidhinā | by pleasing means (pleasing+by a method) |
| Saccaṃ ------------------------------------------ | truth |
| vihāya | discarding |
| matisaccakavādaketuṃ = mati+saccaka+vāda+ketuṃ | wily Saccaka (intended to raise) the banner of his false doctrine (hankering after+Saccaka + false doctrine+banner) |
| vādābhiropitamanaṃ = vāda+abhiropita+manaṃ | with a mind bent upon raising controversies (controversy+bent upon raising+mind) |
| ati-andhabhūtaṃ=ati+andhabhūtaṃ | being completely blinded (extremely+being blinded) |
| paññāpadīpajalito=paññā+padīpa +jalito | by the shining lamp of wisdom (wisdom+lamp + by the shining) |

| | |
|---|---|
| Nandopananda | name of a naga (serpent) |
| bhujagaṃ | serpent |
| vividhaṃ | of different types |
| mahiddhiṃ=mahā+iddhi | great psychic power (great+power) |
| puttena | by the son |
| thera | senior monk |
| bhujagena | by the serpent |
| damāpayanto | caused to be tamed |
| iddhūpadesavidhinā = iddhi+upadesa+vidhinā | by means of psychic powers and advice (psychic powers+advice+by means of) |
| duggāhadiṭṭhibhujagena = duggāha+diṭṭhi+bhujagena snake) | by the snake of deluded views (held wrongly/deluded+views+by the |
| sudaṭṭha-hatthaṃ=su+daṭṭha+hatthaṃ | with hand bitten by (thorough+bitten+hand) |
| brahmaṃ | Brahmā |
| visuddhijutimiddhi=visuddhi+jutiṃ + iddhi | (pure+radiant+powerful) |
| bakābhidhānaṃ.=baka+abhidhānaṃ. | named Baka (baka+named) |
| ñāṇāgadena=ñāṇa+agadena | by the medicine of knowledge (knowledge + medicine) |

## Day - 6

## Paṭiccasamuppāda

| | |
|---|---|
| Paṭicca+samuppādo | dependent, resulting from+origination, arising |
| Anulomaṃ | in direct order |
| Avijjā+paccayā | ignorance+base, foundation, cause |
| saṅkhārā | reactions |
| saṅkhārapaccayā | base of reactions |
| viññāṇaṃ | consciousness |
| nāma-rūpaṃ | mind and body |
| saḷāyatanaṃ | six sense organs |
| phasso | contact |
| vedanā | sensations |
| taṇhā | craving and aversion |
| upādānaṃ | attachment |
| bhavo | process of becoming |
| jāti | birth |
| jarā-maraṇaṃ | ageing and death |
| soka-parideva-dukkha-domanassupāyāsā | sorrow-lamentation-physical suffering-mental suffering, grief |
| sambhavanti | arise |
| Evametassa=evaṃ+etassa | like this (thus+of this) |
| kevalassa | entire |
| dukkhakkhandhassa=dukkha+khandha | mass of suffering (suffering+mass) |
| samudayo | arising |
| Paṭilomaṃ | in reverse order |

| | |
|---|---|
| Avijjāyatveva=Avijjāya+tveva | ignorance+however |
| asesa-virāga-nirodhā=asesa+virāga + nirodhā | complete+eradication of craving + cessation |

## Udāna-gāthā

| | |
|---|---|
| Yadā ------------------------------------------- | when |
| have | surely, indeed |
| pātubhavanti | become manifest |
| dhammā | truths (4 noble) |
| ātāpino | ardently |
| jhāyato | meditating |
| brāhmaṇassa | one of pure life |
| athassa=atha+assa | then his |
| kaṅkhā | doubts |
| vapayanti | disappear |
| sabbā | all |
| yato | because |
| pajānāti | he understands ('pa' for pañña, insight, wisdom) |
| sahetu | with reason |
| khayaṃ | destruction |
| paccayānaṃ | of conditions for arising |
| avedī | he experiences |
| vidhūpayaṃ | having scattered |
| tiṭṭhati | he stands |
| mārasenaṃ | army of Māra |
| sūriyova | sun-like |
| obhāsayamantalikkhaṃ | shining in the sky |
| Aneka------------------------------------------- | countless |
| jāti | birth |
| saṃsāraṃ | faring on (cycle of existence) |
| sandhāvissaṃ | I have run |
| anibbisaṃ. | in vain, not finding |
| Gahakāraṃ | builder of this house |
| gavesanto | seeking |
| dukkhā | suffering |
| punappunaṃ. | again and again |
| Gahakāraka------------------------------------ | housebuilder |
| diṭṭhosi | you are seen |
| puna | again |
| gehaṃ | house |
| na | not |
| kāhasi | will build |
| te | your |
| phāsukā | beams |
| bhaggā | broken |
| gahakūṭaṃ | ridge pole (central pillar) |
| visaṅkhitaṃ. | shattered |

| | |
|---|---|
| visaṅkhāragataṃ=visaṅkhāra+gataṃ | free from conditioning+gone to/arrived at |
| cittaṃ | mind |
| taṇhānaṃ | craving (of) |
| khayamajjhagā=khayaṃ+ajjhagā | end/cessation+reached |
| Jayo ------------------------------------------- | victory |
| hi | yes, indeed |
| buddhassa | of Buddha |
| sirīmato | glorious |
| ayaṃ | this (person) |
| mārassa | of Māra |
| ca | and |
| pāpimato | sinful |
| parājayo | defeat |
| ugghosayuṃ | these were proclaimed |
| bodhimaṇḍe | from the seat of enlightenment |
| pamoditā | rejoicing |
| jayaṃ | victory |
| tadā | then, at that time |
| nāga-gaṇā | host, multitude of nāgas |
| mahesino | of great sage (the Buddha) |
| supaṇṇa-gaṇā | host of garudas (mythical bird) |
| devagaṇā | host of devas |
| brahma-gaṇā | host of brahmas |

## Day 7

## Bojjhaṅgaparitta

| | |
|---|---|
| Saṃsāre ---------------------------------------- | cycle of birth and death (in this world) |
| saṃsarantānaṃ | (for those beings) transmigrating |
| sabbadukkhavināsake=sabba+dukkha + vināsake | eradicating all suffering (all+suffering + eradicating) |
| satta+dhamme | seven+factors |
| ca | and |
| bojjhaṅge | factors of enlightenment |
| mārasenappamaddane=māra+sena + pamaddane | defeating the army of Māra (māra+army + defeating) |
| Bujjhitvā -------------------------------------- | realizing |
| ye cime=ye+ca+ime | which+and+these |
| sattā | beings |
| tibhavā | 3 types of existence (kāma, rūpa, arūpa) |
| muttakuttamā=muttaka+uttamā | liberated+excellent ones |
| ajātiṃ | free from birth |
| ajarābyādhiṃ=ajāra+byādhiṃ | free from decay/old age+sickness |
| amataṃ | deathless |
| nibbhayaṃ | fearlessness |
| gatā | gone (experienced the stage) |
| Evamādi=Evaṃ+ādi -------------------------- | like these+etc. |

| | |
|---|---|
| guṇūpetaṃ=guṇa+upetaṃ (merit+endowed) | endowed with such advantages |
| anekaguṇasaṅgahaṃ.=aneka+guṇa + saṅgahaṃ. | innumerable+merit/benefit+collection |
| osadhañca | medicine |
| imaṃ | this |
| mantaṃ | words, incantation |
| bhaṇāmahe | let us recite |
| sati+saṅkhāto---------------------------------- | awareness+so called/namely |
| dhammānaṃ-vicayo | analytical investigation of Dhamma |
| tathā likewise | |
| vīriyaṃ | effort |
| pīti | joy |
| passaddhi | tranquillity |
| pare | after, others, the rest |
| Samādhupekkhā=samādhi+upekkhā ------- | concentration+equanimity |
| sattete=satta+ete | these seven (seven+these) |
| sabbadassinā | by the all-seeing |
| muninā | sage |
| sammadakkhātā | well-taught, preached |
| bhāvitā | cultivated |
| bahulīkatā | practiced frequently |
| Saṃvattanti ------------------------------------ | lead to, conduce to |
| abhiññāya | higher knowledge, supernormal power (to) |
| nibbānāya | liberation (to) |
| bodhiyā | enlightenment (to) |
| etena | by this |
| saccavajjena=sacca+vajja | by this true utterance (truth+utterance) |
| sotthi | happiness, well-being |
| te | your |
| hotu | may be |
| sabbadā | always |
| Ekasmiṃ --------------------------------------- | at one |
| samaye | time |
| nātho | the lord, protector |
| moggalānañca=moggalāna+ca | Moggallāna and |
| kassapaṃ | Kassapa (names of disciples of the Buddha) |
| gilāne | sick |
| dukkhite | suffering |
| disvā | seeing |
| desayī | preached |
| taṃ ------------------------------------------- | this, that |
| abhinanditvā | rejoicing |
| rogā | from sickness |
| muccimsu | became free |
| taṅkhaṇe | at that very moment |

| | |
|---|---|
| Ekadā ------------------------------------------ | once |
| dhammarājāpi | king of Dhamma also |
| gelaññenābhipīḷito=gelaññena+abhipīḷito | afflicted by sickness (by sickness+afflicted) |
| cundattherena | the elder Cunda (by) |
| taṃ yeva | the same |
| bhaṇāpetvāna | having caused to recite |
| sādaraṃ. | with reverence |
| Sammoditvāna ------------------------------- | having rejoiced |
| ābādhā | from disease |
| tamhā | from that |
| vuṭṭhāsi | rose up |
| ṭhānaso | causally, with reason |
| Pahīnā ------------------------------------------ | eliminated |
| tiṇṇannampi | for these three |
| mahesinaṃ. | of great sages |
| maggāhatā | the path destroys |
| kilesā'va | defilements |
| pattānupatti=patta+anupatti | attained/reached+attainment |
| dhammataṃ. | nature, law |

## Day 8

## Mittānisaṃsa

| | |
|---|---|
| Pūrento ---------------------------------------- | while fulfilling |
| bodhisambhāre | necessary conditions for enlightenment |
| nātho | the lord |
| Temiya | name of the prince |
| jātiyaṃ. | in his birth |
| mittānisaṃsaṃ (= mitta+ānisaṃsaṃ) | friend(ship)+advantage, reward, merit |
| yaṃ | which |
| āha | spoke |
| sunanda | name of charioteer |
| nāma | named |
| sārathiṃ. | charioteer |
| sabbalokahitatthāya=Sabba+loka+hita (all+world+benefit+ atthāya | for the benefit of all the world + for the purpose) |
| parittaṃ | protective verse |
| taṃ | that |
| bhaṇāmahe | let us recite |
| Pahūtabhakkho------------------------------- | a person well-feasted |
| bhavati | is |
| vippavuttho | out of, absent from |
| sakā | one's own |
| gharā | (from) house |
| bahūnaṃ | many |
| upajīvanti | depend upon him |
| yo | whosoever |
| mittānaṃ | friends |

| | |
|---|---|
| na | not |
| dūbhati (var. of dubbhati) | betray, deceive |
| Yaṃyaṃ---------------------------------------- | whichever (which+that/which) |
| janapadaṃ | land, province |
| yāti | he goes |
| nigame | small town |
| rājadhāniyo | or royal city |
| sabbattha | everywhere |
| pūjito | honored |
| hoti | is |
| Nāssa=Na+assa-------------------------------- | not+him |
| corā | thieves |
| pasahanti | overpower |
| nātimaññeti=na+atimaññeti | not despised (do not+despise) |
| khattiyo | a warrior, prince, ruler |
| sabbe | all |
| amitte | enemies |
| tarati | overcomes, crosses |
| Akuddho -------------------------------------- | not angry |
| sagharaṃ=sa+gharaṃ | to his house (own+house) |
| eti | comes, returns |
| sabhāya | assembly |
| paṭinandito | welcome |
| ñātīnaṃ | relatives |
| uttamo | eminent |
| Sakkatvā ------------------------------------- | being hospitable |
| sakkato | receiver of hospitality |
| garu | he is esteemed |
| sagāravo | esteeming others, respectful |
| vaṇṇakittibhato = Vaṇṇa+kitti+bhato | one who receives praise and fame (praise+fame+bearing) |
| Pūjako ---------------------------------------- | respecting others |
| labhate | receives, gains |
| pūjaṃ | respect |
| vandako | honoring others |
| paṭivandanaṃ.=paṭi+vandanaṃ. | he is honored (in return+[he gets] honor) |
| yaso | fame |
| kittiñca | fame |
| pappoti | attains |
| Aggi ------------------------------------------ | fire |
| yathā | like |
| pajjalati | shines forth |
| devatāva=devatā+va | celestial being+like |
| virocati | he is radiant, he shines forth |
| siriyā | fortune |
| ajahito | not abandoned |
| Gāvo ------------------------------------------ | cattle |
| tassa | his |
| pajāyanti | multiply, increase |

| | |
|---|---|
| khette | in the field |
| vuttaṃ | what is sown |
| virūhati | grows |
| vuttānaṃ | whatever is sown |
| phalamasnāti=phalaṃ+asnāti | he enjoys the fruit (fruit+eats, enjoys) |
| Darito------------------------------------------ | from the cleft (cavity) |
| pabbatato | from a mountain |
| vā | or |
| rukkhato | from a tree |
| patito | fallen |
| naro | man |
| cuto | when fallen |
| patiṭṭhaṃ | firm footing, help, support |
| labhati | finds |
| Virūḷhamūlasantānaṃ=Virūḷha + mūla+santānaṃ ------------ | which has its roots spread out far (grown+root+succession, spreading, continuity) |
| nigrodhamiva=nigrodhaṃ+iva | banyan tree like (banyan tree+like) |
| māluto | from wind |
| amittā | enemies |
| pasahanti | overpower |

## Day 9

## Maṅgala Suttaṃ

| | |
|---|---|
| Yaṃ ------------------------------------------ | which |
| maṅgalaṃ | blessing, auspiciousness, prosperity |
| dvādasahi | for twelve (years) |
| cintayiṃsu | thought over |
| sadevakā | along with the devas |
| sotthānaṃ | blessings, prosperity |
| nādhigacchanti=na+adhigacchanti | not get at (do not+arrive at) |
| aṭṭhatiṃsañca | thirty-eight |
| Desitaṃ ---------------------------------------- | taught |
| devadevena | highest celestial being |
| sabbapāpavināsanaṃ=sabba+pāpa + vināsanaṃ | will destroy all evil (all+evil + destruction) |
| sabbaloka-hitatthāya=sabba+loka+hita (all+world+benefit | for the benefit of all the world + for the purpose) |
| taṃ | that |
| bhaṇāmahe | let us recite |
| Evaṃ------------------------------------------ | thus |
| me | by me |
| sutaṃ | has been heard |
| ekaṃ | one, certain |
| samayaṃ | time, occasion |
| bhagavā | the exalted one |
| sāvatthiyaṃ | in Sāvatthi (a city) |

| | |
|---|---|
| viharati | dwelling |
| jetavane | in Jetavana (Jeta's grove) |
| anāthapiṇḍikassa | of Anāthapiṇḍika (a lay disciple of the Buddha) |
| ārāme | monastery |
| atha | then |
| kho | indeed |
| aññatarā | someone, a certain |
| devatā (fem.) | deity (female) |
| abhikkantāya | advanced |
| rattiyā | night |
| abhikkantavaṇṇā=abhikkanta+vaṇṇā | of beautiful complexion (surpassing+beauty) |
| kevalakappaṃ | the whole of it |
| jetavanaṃ | the Jeta grove |
| obhāsetvā | illuminating |
| yena | where |
| tenupasaṅkami=tena+upasaṅkami | there+went/approached |
| upasaṅkamitvā | having gone there |
| bhagavantaṃ | the exalted one |
| abhivādetvā | saluting |
| ekamantaṃ | one side |
| aṭṭhāsi | stood |
| ṭhitā | standing |
| sā | she |
| gāthāya | in verse |
| ajjhabhāsi | addressed, spoke out |
| Bahū ------------------------------------------- | many |
| devā | gods |
| manussā | men |
| ca | also, too |
| maṅgalāni | blessings, welfare, good |
| acintayuṃ | thought over |
| ākaṅkhamānā | wishing for |
| brūhi | you tell |
| maṅgalamuttamaṃ=maṅgalaṃ + uttamaṃ | highest welfare (welfare+highest, best) |
| Asevanā ---------------------------------------- | avoidance, no association with |
| bālānaṃ | fools (of) |
| paṇḍitānaṃ | wise ones |
| sevanā | associate with |
| pūjā | honor |
| pūjanīyānaṃ | who should be honored |
| Patirūpa+desavāso ---------------------------- | suitable, proper+region, country |
| pubbe | past |
| katapuññatā=kata+puññatā | merit of past good deeds (done+good deeds) |
| atta-sammāpaṇidhi=atta+sammā+paṇidhi | self+right+aspiration |
| Bāhusaccañca=Bāhu+saccaṃ+ca ----------- | great learning (great+truth+and) |
| sippaṃ | skill |
| vinayo | discipline |

| | |
|---|---|
| susikkhito | well-mastered |
| subhāsitā=su+bhāsitā | well-spoken (well+spoken) |
| yā | those |
| vācā | words, speech |
| Mātā-pitu---------------------------------------- | mother-father |
| upaṭṭhānaṃ | serving |
| puttadārassa | children and spouse |
| saṅgaho | caring, tending |
| anākulā=an+ākulā | simple(not+entangled, twisted) |
| kammantā | occupation |
| Dānaṃ+ca ------------------------------------ | generosity+and |
| dhammacariyā | life of dhamma |
| ñātakānaṃ | relatives |
| anavajjāni | blameless |
| kammāni | deeds |
| Āratī ------------------------------------------ | abstinence |
| viratī | shunning |
| pāpā | evil |
| majjapānā | consuming liquor and intoxicants |
| saṃyamo | refraining |
| appamādo | vigilance, carefulness |
| dhammesu | in Dhamma |
| Gāravo------------------------------------------ | respectfulness |
| nivāto | humility |
| santuṭṭhi | contentment |
| kataññutā | gratefulness |
| kālena | proper time |
| dhammassavanaṃ | hearing the Dhamma |
| Khantī ------------------------------------------ | forbearance, tolerance |
| sovacassatā | amenability to instruction, surrender, obedience |
| samaṇānaṃ | saintly people |
| dassanaṃ | visiting, beholding |
| dhammasākacchā | discussions about Dhamma |
| Tapo -------------------------------------------- | ardent practice |
| brahmacariyaṃ | holy life, abstinence |
| ariyasaccāna-dassanaṃ=ariya+saccānaṃ + dassanaṃ | witnessing the noble truths (noble+of truths + witnessing) |
| nibbānasacchikiriyā=nibbāna + sacchikiriyā | experiencing nibbāna (nibbāna + experience) |
| Phuṭṭhassa--------------------------------------- | facing, confronted with, coming in contact with |
| lokadhammehi=loka+dhammehi | dhammas of the world (world+by dhammas/ conditions) |
| cittaṃ | mind |
| yassa | whose |
| na | not |
| kampati | trembles, shakes |
| asokaṃ | free from sorrow |
| virajaṃ | free from defilements |

| | |
|---|---|
| khemaṃ | secure |
| Etādisāni -------------------------------------- | this way |
| katvāna | having acted |
| sabbatthamaparājitā=sabbathaṃ+aparājitā | everywhere+undefeated |
| sabbatthasotthiṃ=sabbattha+sotthiṃ | everywhere+in safety |
| gacchanti | they go |

## Day 10

## Mettā-Bhāvanā

| | |
|---|---|
| Ahaṃ | I |
| avero | free from animosity |
| homi | may I be |
| abyāpajjho | free from aversion |
| Anīgho=an+īgha | undisturbed (not+trembling, disturbed) |
| sukhī | happy |
| attānaṃ | myself |
| pariharāmi | to take care of, protect, shelter |
| Mātā-pitu-ācariya-ñāti-samūhā -------------- | mother - father - teacher - relatives - multitude (mass, aggregation) |
| hontu | may they be |
| Ārakkhadevatā -------------------------------- | guardian deities |
| bhūmaṭṭhadevatā | earth-bound deities |
| rukkhaṭṭhadevatā | tree-bound deities |
| ākāsaṭṭhadevatā | sky-bound deities |
| Puratthimāya ---------------------------------- | east |
| disāya | direction |
| anudisāya | middle-direction |
| Dakkhiṇāya | south |
| Pacchimāya | west |
| Uttarāya | north |
| Uparimāya | above |
| heṭṭhimāya | below |
| Sabbe ------------------------------------------ | all |
| sattā | beings |
| pāṇā | living |
| bhūtā | creatures |
| puggalā | individuals |
| attabhāvapariyāpannā | having any form of life |
| itthiyo | females, women |
| purisā | males, men |
| ariyā | who have attained purity of mind |
| anariyā | who have not attained purity of mind |
| manussā | men, humans |
| amanussā | non-humans |
| devā | gods |
| vinipātikā | in states of woe (hell) |

| | |
|---|---|
| ca | also, too, and |
| khemino | secure |
| bhadrāṇi | fortune, auspiciousness |
| passantu | see |
| mā | do not (prohibitive particle) |
| kiñci | something |
| pāpamāgamā | encounter evil |
| dukkhamāgamā | encounter grief |

## Pāli from Adhiṭṭhāna ending chanting *[pages 68 - 69]*

*Most of the verses presented here also occur in the Pāli Passages from the Evening Discourses. See page 78-79.*

| | |
|---|---|
| Anicca | impermanent |
| vata | indeed, truly |
| saṅkhārā | compounded (conditioned) things/ phenomena |
| uppādavayadhammino= | having the nature of arising and passing away |
| (uppāda+vaya+dhammino) | (arising+passing away+the nature of) |
| uppajjitvā | having arisen |
| nirujjhanti | (they) get eradicated, cease |
| tesaṃ | their |
| vūpasamo | cessation |
| sukho | (is) happiness |

*[For word meanings for Aneka-jāti-saṃsāraṃ . . . see page 102]*

| | |
|---|---|
| Sabbe | all |
| yadā | when |
| paññāya | with wisdom/insight |
| passati | sees, perceives |
| atha | then |
| nibbindati | gets weary/disgusted |
| dukkhe | (toward) suffering |
| esa | this (is) |
| maggo | path |
| visuddhiyā | (of) purification |

| | |
|---|---|
| Yato yato | whenever, wherever |
| (yato) | (since, whence) |
| sammasati | grasps/understands/knows thoroughly |
| khandhānaṃ | of the aggregates |
| udayabbayaṃ | rise and fall, arising and passing away |
| labhatī | gets, experiences |
| pīti | rapture, ecstasy |
| pāmojjaṃ | bliss, delight |
| amataṃ | deathless stage (acc.) |
| taṃ | that |
| vijānataṃ | understood |

## Puññānumodanaṃ *[page 69]*

| | |
|---|---|
| Puññānumodanaṃ=puñña + anumodanaṃ | merit+approval, acceptance, giving thanks |
| Sabbesu---------------------------------------- | (in) all |
| cakkavāḷesu | world systems |
| yakkhā | nonhuman beings, demons |
| devā | devas |
| ca | and |
| brahmuno | brahmās |
| Yaṃ | whatever |
| amhehi | by us |
| kataṃ | done |
| puññaṃ | merit |
| sabbasampatti=sabba+sampatti | all kinds of prosperity (all+prosperity) |
| sādhakaṃ. | bringing about |
| Sabbe ------------------------------------------ | all |
| taṃ | that |
| anumoditvā | having rejoiced |
| samaggā | unitedly |
| sāsane | to teaching |
| ratā | devoted |
| pamādarahitā=pamāda+rahitā | without negligence (negligence+without) |
| hontu | may they be |
| ārakkhāsu | in giving protection |
| visesato | especially |
| Puññabhāgamidaṃ=Puñña + bhāgaṃ+idaṃ ----------------- | merit+portion+this |
| c'aññaṃ=ca+aññaṃ | and before (and+other) |
| samaṃ | equally |
| dadāma | give |
| kāritaṃ | I have done |
| anumodantu | accept with joy |
| medinī | the earth |
| ṭhātu | stay, remain, stand |
| sakkhike | witness |

## Pāli from the Discourses

*Many passages from the discourses are taken from the suttas in the morning chanting. Sutta references are given in the chapter 'Pāli Passages Quoted in the Discourses'. Please refer to the appropriate sutta section for the word meanings of these verses. See also page 110, 'Pāli from Adhiṭṭhāna ending chanting' for those verses that also occur in the Pāli from the discourses .*

*[page 77]*

| | |
|---|---|
| Tumhehi---------------------------------------- | by you |
| kiccaṃ | work |
| ātappaṃ | exertion |
| akkhātāro | expounders, preachers |
| tathāgatā | Enlightened Ones |
| | |
| Sabba-pāpassa---------------------------------- | (of) all unwholesome/unvirtuous actions |
| akaraṇaṃ | non-doing, not doing |
| kusalassa | (of ) wholesome/virtuous actions |
| upasampadā | acquiring/acquisition |
| sa-citta | ones' own mind |
| pariyodapanaṃ | purification, cleansing |
| etaṃ | this |
| Buddhāna | of the Buddhas |
| sāsanaṃ | teaching, doctrine, order |
| | |
| Niccaṃ ----------------------------------------- | always |
| kāyagatā-sati | awareness related to the body |
| = kāyagatā+sati | (relating to the body+awareness) |
| | |
| Mano ------------------------------------------- | mind |
| pubbaṅgamā | forerunner, precursor |
| dhammā | (all) phenomena |
| mano-seṭṭhā | mind is chief |
| mano-mayā | mind-made |
| manasā | (with) mind |
| ce | if |
| paduṭṭhena | (with) bad/impure |
| bhāsati | speaks |
| vā | or |
| karoti | does, acts |
| tato | then, thence |
| naṃ | him/her |
| dukkhamanveti=dukkhaṃ+anveti | suffering follows (suffering+follows) |
| cakkaṃ'va=cakkaṃ+va | like a cartwheel (wheel+like) |
| vahato | draught animal, carrier |
| padaṃ | foot |
| pasannena-------------------------------------- | (with) good/pure |
| sukhamanveti=sukhaṃ+anveti | happiness follows (happiness+follows) |
| chāyā'va=chāyā+va | like a shadow (shadow+like) |
| anapāyinī=an+apāyinī | constantly following (not+going away) |

*[page 78]*

| | |
|---|---|
| Jāti ------------------------------------------- | birth |
| pi | also (emphatic particle) |

| | |
|---|---|
| dukkhā | suffering |
| jarā | decay/old age |
| vyādhi | sickness |
| maraṇaṃ | death |
| dukkhaṃ | suffering |
| appiyehi | (with) unpleasant |
| sampayogo | association |
| dukkho | suffering |
| piyehi | (from) pleasant |
| vippayogo | dissociation/separation |
| yam'p'icchaṃ=yaṃ+pi+icchaṃ | what one wants/desires (that+also+desired thing) |
| na | not |
| labhati | to get, gets |
| tam'pi=taṃ+pi | is also (that+also) |
| saṅkhittena | in short, concisely |
| pañc'upādānakkhandhā = pañca+upādāna+khandhā | attachment to the five aggregates (five+clinging/ attachment+aggregates) |

*[page 79]*

| | |
|---|---|
| Sabbadānaṃ ---------- | all gifts |
| dhammadānaṃ | the gift of dhamma |
| jināti | overpowers, excels |
| sabbarasaṃ | all flavors |
| dhammaraso | the flavor/taste of dhamma |
| sabbaratiṃ | all delights |
| dhammarati | delight in dhamma |
| taṇhakkhayo | destruction of craving |
| sabbadukkhaṃ | all suffering |

*[page 81]*

| | |
|---|---|
| Pakārena ---------- | (by) different ways |
| jānāti | knows |
| (i)ti | quotation marker |
| paññā | wisdom |

*[page 82]*

| | |
|---|---|
| Atta-dīpā=atta+dīpa ---------- | island of oneself (oneself+island) |
| viharatha | dwell |
| atta-saraṇā | refuge in oneself |
| anaññasaraṇā=an+añña+saraṇā | no other refuge (no+other+refuge) |
| dhamma-dīpā | island of Dhamma |
| dhamma-saraṇā | refuge of Dhamma |

## Bibliography

Goenka, S. N. *Come People of the World.* Igatpuri, India: Vipassana Research Institute, 1999.

Goenka, S. N. *Dhamma Verses*. Seattle: Vipassana Research Publications, 2000.

Goenka, S. N.; Hart, William, ed. *Discourse Summaries*. Igatpuri, India: Vipassana Research Institute, 1987.

Goenka, S. N. and others. *Vipassana Journal.* Hyderabad, India: Vipassana Vishodhana Vinyas, 1985.

Hart, William. *The Art of Living.* Igatpuri, India: Vipassana Research Institute, 1991.

K Sri Dhammananda. Ven. *Daily Buddhist Devotions.* Kuala Lumpur, Malaysia: Buddhist Missionary Society, 1993.

Ledi Sayadaw, Ven. *Manuals of Dhamma.* Igatpuri, India: Vipassana Research Institute, 1999.

Lokuliyana, Lionel. *The Great Book of Protections: Sinhala Mahā Pirit Pota*. Colombo, Sri Lanka, Mrs. H. M. Gunasekara Trust Fund.

Nārada Thera, Bhikkhu Kassapa. *Mirror of the Dhamma* (Wheel Publication no. 54). Kandy, Sri Lanka: Buddhist Publication Society, 1984.

Nyanatiloka Thera. *The Buddha's Path to Deliverance*. Seattle: BPS Pariyatti Editions, 2002.

Nyanatiloka Thera. *Buddhist Dictionary.* Kandy, Sri Lanka: Buddhist Publication Society, 1980.

Piyadassi Thera. *The Book of Protection*. Kuala Lumpur: Buddhist Missionary Society, 1980.

Saddhatissa, Ven. H. *The Sutta Nipāta*. Richmond, Surrey, UK: Curzon Press, 1994.

Soni, Dr. R.L. *Life's Highest Blessings* (Wheel Publication no. 254/256). Kandy, Sri Lanka: Buddhist Publication Society, 1987.

Story, Francis and Vajirā, Sister, trans. *The Last Days of the Buddha*. Kandy, Sri Lanka: Buddhist Publication Society, 1998

U Ba Khin, Sayagyi; Goenka, S.N. and others. *Sayagyi U Ba Khin Journal.* Igatpuri, India: Vipassana Research Institute, 1999.

U Sīlānandabhivaṃsa, Sayadaw. *Paritta Pāli and Protective Verses.* Yangon, Myanmar: International Theravāda Buddhist Missionary University, 2001

## ABOUT VIPASSANA

Courses of Vipassana meditation as taught by S.N. Goenka in the tradition of Sayagyi U Ba Khin are held regularly in many countries around the world.

Information, worldwide schedules and application forms are available from the Vipassana website: *www.dhamma.org*

## ABOUT PARIYATTI

Pariyatti is dedicated to providing affordable access to authentic teachings of the Buddha about the Dhamma theory (*pariyatti*) and practice (*paṭipatti*) of Vipassana meditation. A 501(c)(3) non-profit charitable organization since 2002, Pariyatti is sustained by contributions from individuals who appreciate and want to share the incalculable value of the Dhamma teachings. We invite you to visit *www.pariyatti.org* to learn about our programs, services, and ways to support publishing and other undertakings.

### Pariyatti Publishing Imprints

***Vipassana Research Publications*** (focus on Vipassana as taught by S.N. Goenka in the tradition of Sayagyi U Ba Khin)

***BPS Pariyatti Editions*** (selected titles from the Buddhist Publication Society, co-published by Pariyatti)

***MPA Pariyatti Editions*** (selected titles from the Myanmar Pitaka Association, co-published by Pariyatti)

***Pariyatti Digital Editions*** (audio and video titles, including discourses)

***Pariyatti Press*** (classic titles returned to print and inspirational writing by contemporary authors)

### Pariyatti enriches the world by

- disseminating the words of the Buddha,
- providing sustenance for the seeker's journey,
- illuminating the meditator's path.

Printed in Great Britain
by Amazon

44914011R00074